Understanding Our New United Methodist Hymnal

Understanding Our New United Methodist Hymnal

by Riley B. Case

BRISTOL
BOOKS

UNDERSTANDING OUR NEW UNITED METHODIST HYMNAL
© by Riley B. Case
Published by Bristol Books

First Edition, May 1989
Second Printing, November 1989

Unless otherwise indicated all Scripture quotations are from the *Holy Bible*, the New International Version, © 1973, 1978, 1984 by International Bible Society. Used by permission.

Scripture quotations indicated (RSV) are from the Revised Standard Bible © 1946, 1952, 1971 by the Division of Christian Education of the National Council of the Church of Christ in the U.S.A. Used by permission.

Grateful acknowledgement is made to the following who have granted permission for the reprinting of lines from copyrighted material:

John B. Geyer, for "We Know that Christ Is Raised." Copyright, John B. Geyer.
Gaither Copyright Management, Alexandria, IN 46001, for "He Touched Me."
Oxford University Press, 200 Madison Ave., New York 10016, for "Source and Sovereign, Rock and Cloud," by Thomas H. Troeger.
Abingdon Press, for "Wash, O God, Our Sons and Daughters." Words copyright 1989 by the United Methodist Publishing House. From *The United Methodist Hymnal*. Reprinted by permission.
Hope Publishing Company, for "Great Is Thy Faithfulness." Copyright 1923. Renewal 1951 by Hope Publishing Company, Carol Stream, IL 60188. All rights reserved. Used by permission.
The Lorenz Publishing Company, Box 802 Dayton, OH 45401, for verse three of "This Is My Song," by Georgia Harkness. Used by permission.
Manna Music, Inc., 25510 Avenue Stanford, Valencia, CA 91355, for "The Blood Will Never Lose Its Power," by Andre Crouch and "How Great Thou Art."

Library of Congress Card Number: 89-60520
ISBN: 0-917851-31-5
Suggested Subject Headings:
1. Hymn Stories
2. The United Methodist Hymnal
Recommended Dewey Decimal Classification: 783.952

BRISTOL BOOKS
An imprint of Good News, a Forum for Scriptural Christianity, Inc.
308 East Main Street • Wilmore, Kentucky 40390

Contents

To the churches of the Marion District,
where old Methodist songs are loved and sung

Preface

Who are the United Methodists? A most diverse group, they are liberal and conservative, black and white, Asian-American, Hispanic, Native American, feminist and traditionalist. They are professors in universities, farmers in rural areas and teachers in small towns. Geographically, they range from New England to the deep South to Alaska and even overseas. Their theological differences are even more pronounced, ranging from liberalism scarcely distinguishable from Unitarianism to fundamentalism. United Methodists attend large city churches of twelve thousand members and small country churches of twenty members. Some of those churches were once United Brethren, others were from the Evangelical Church and still others were Methodist Protestant, Methodist Episcopal North and Methodist Episcopal South.

United Methodists can be studied many different ways. One could read the United Methodist *Discipline* (a method that is normally not very exciting). One could summarize what is taught in the denomination's seminaries or examine the pronouncements of its boards and agencies. One could read United Methodist history or compile statistics on churches and membership—by age or size or geographical location.

This study takes a different approach. It looks at United Methodism by examining its hymns. Our primary focus will be on the new 1989 United Methodist hymnal, but we will also review the traditions and background that brought us to the new hymnal. This study is not intended to be an introduction to the hymnal (other materials will do that) nor a treatise on hymnology or worship. It is an attempt to discover who United Methodists are by understanding what we have sung and why we have sung it and what we sing today.

In addition, it is hoped this study can help us in our Christian walk by focusing on the essential doctrines of the faith and on our theological and cultural heritage.

The purposes of this volume are:

1. To explore United Methodist doctrine, history and tradition through a study of hymns and the new hymnal;

2. To gain an appreciation for biblical images in the hymns of the church and learn how we can make use of these images in our worship to appropriate and interpret scriptural truths;

3. To seek a realization of who we are as a people and of the contributions various groups have made to our life together. Particular emphasis is given to that portion of the church known as "evangelical," including revivalism and the camp meeting movement; and

4. To become sensitive to contemporary issues in the church by understanding how those issues have been dealt with in our hymns.

Following are several presuppositions from which this study is written:

• The term "Methodist" as used in this study includes the traditions of all the former denominations which now comprise the United Methodist Church. These earlier denominations' common tradition can be traced from the challenge of modern liberalism back through frontier revivalism and camp meetings to the influence of the Wesleys and the Wesleyan awakening in England. At the same time references to official hymnals (unless otherwise noted) indicate hymnals of the Methodist or Methodist Episcopal Church. Such hymnals were issued in 1848, 1878, 1905, 1935 and 1966.

• United Methodists are part of the evangelical Christian world, historically, culturally and theologically. They have not abandoned that perspective nearly as much as some would have us believe.

• Methodism has played a major role in defining modern American Protestantism, including the evangelical movement, and American gospel hymnody.

• The best place to find the heart and soul of United Methodism today is not necessarily in the seminaries and the boards and agencies, but in local churches, in the worship life and the singing of rank-and-file church members.

• The story of common, ordinary believers—the songs they wrote, compiled and sang, particularly songs of the camp meetings and revivals—is often neglected in annals of United Methodist music. However, this story needs to be told. If camp meeting and gospel music seems to receive undue emphasis in this study, it is only to serve as a balance to other studies which tend to neglect this tradition entirely.

• The future hope for United Methodism lies not so much in its ability to be modern, relevant and accommodating to the secular world view, but in its proclaiming with faithfulness the historic, ever-relevant faith which has the power to change lives.

• The kind of hymns we sing and how we sing them will help determine the church's success or failure in proclaiming that historic faith.

One

Can United Methodists Agree on a Hymnal?

Be not dismayed whate'er betide, God will take care of
you;
beneath his wings of love abide, God will take care of
you.
God will take care of you, through every day, o'er all the
way;
he will take care of you, God will take care of you.
(United Methodist Hymnal #130)

"This is doggerel; this hymn should be deleted."

That, as I remember it, was the opening statement as the hymn "Be Not Dismayed Whate'er Betide" was discussed in the Language/Theology subcommittee of the Hymnal Revision Committee for the new 1989 United Methodist hymnal.

Sixteen of us were present on that occasion. In addition to regular members of the committee, several "consultants" (including myself) had been added. It was a knowledgeable, dedicated and opinionated group. Two of these persons had already edited denominational hymnals. One man was a well-known United Methodist theologian who had written a book on hymnody. Also present were four professors, a lawyer, a black music teacher, the head of a large university's school of music and professional organists, including the president of the Fellowship of United Methodist Musicians. Several individuals had strong convictions about the importance of "inclusive language" in the hymnal.

The subcommittee's task was to discuss the appropriateness of the language and theology of hymns being considered for the hymnal. Did a particular hymn meet the language guidelines developed by the committee? Was the theology of the hymn consistent with United Methodist theology and its Social Principles?

The hymnal committee felt that decisions made about the hymnal would help determine the future direction of the church. For United Methodists, the hymnal represents the Book of Common Prayer; it is a Statement of Faith and it also reflects denominational culture and ethos. In a denomination of diverse (some would say fractured) theology, geography and racial and cultural make-up, the hymnal would (it was hoped) provide a symbol of unity. At least all United Methodists would have a common worship book and hymnal, despite their differences.

As it turned out, almost every issue facing United Methodism was confronted in one way or another through the process of preparing the new hymnal: geographical preferences, liberal versus evangelical theology, the traditions of the former denominations (United Brethren, Evangelical Church, Methodist), social issues (racism, militarism, imperialism, nationalism), culture (good music versus popular music) and always, and perhaps especially, the issue of "inclusive language" and all its implications.

Many of those differences seemed to surface in the discussion of the hymn "Be Not Dismayed." It was considered early in the hymn selection process and some of the arguments involved were being made for the first time (later the positions were understood and it was not necessary to repeat the same arguments over and over). The person who declared that the hymn was doggerel and should be deleted went on to suggest that it did not meet the standards of a good hymn.

That comment was countered with the remark, "But this is a favorite hymn of many—it cannot be deleted." A third person quoted from hymnal research already conducted, "According to the church usage survey, seventy-seven percent of United Methodist churches sing the hymn."

Weightier arguments soon followed. A seminary professor spoke against the hymn because of its poor theology.

> *All you may need he will provide,*
> *God will take care of you;*
> *nothing you ask will be denied,*
> *God will take care of you.*

"Look at what the hymn says. This is not only sentimental, but false. It is not always true," he explained, "that nothing you ask will be denied, or that God will always take care of you." He gave some examples of people who asked for something in prayer and did not receive what they asked for. He also mentioned starving children in Africa to illustrate that God does not always provide even basic necessities such as food.

A black woman spoke: "In the black church people do not want songs that say God may or may not take care of them. They want a positive message that, whatever it means, or however it may happen, God will come to their rescue."

Then someone mentioned that song's message is based on Psalm 91. The question was asked, Is the hymn faithful to the message of Psalm 91?

> *For he will deliver you from the snare of the fowler*
> *and from the deadly pestilence;*
> *he will cover you with his pinions,*
> *and under his wings you will find refuge. . . .*
> (Psalm 91:3,4, RSV)

In true United Methodist style, there were, obviously, two answers to the question: yes and no. Yes, God takes care of his children. It may not be in the way we expect, but the care is there and God is working his will in us. The other reply was no, God cares for his children but does not grant our every wish. Suffering and pain exist in the world; we create unrealistic expectations if we teach that God fulfills our every need. Whatever Psalm 91 means, it does not mean that.

The discussion was by no means over. A committee member observed that the hymn is individualistic and privatistic. It would have me be concerned only about myself, not the needs of others. It does not hold me accountable to my responsibilities before God.

Another woman spoke a personal word. She had recently lost

her husband and noted that in a time of helplessness "sometimes we cannot do anything; it helps to know God is there."

The discussion continued. A woman raised the question of all the male pronouns the hymn uses to refer to God. If for no other reason than the excessive masculine language, she thought the hymn should be deleted or at least changed. She was answered by another woman who said, "But the hymn was written by a woman—and we need hymns by women—and stresses God's nurturing, feminine qualities." She pointed out that "Beneath his wings of love" is not the image of a rooster but of a mother hen. "Lean, weary one, upon his breast" describes a nurturing side of God that women want to emphasize.

The same woman, who came from a Lutheran background, continued: "This hymn is not in any Lutheran hymnal. It does not meet my objective standards for good music or a good text. But when my Lutheran grandmother was dying, this was the hymn she wanted sung to her. What I remember about it at the time was the extravagance—more than what made good sense—of God's love and care that was promised."

She paused and admitted she knew the hymn by memory.

The final vote was taken to decide whether to recommend the hymn to the larger committee: Seven people voted to keep the hymn; four voted to delete it; and one person abstained. The committee members turned the pages of their workbooks and started discussing the next hymn.

The debate surrounding that one hymn, "Be Not Dismayed," was not untypical of many discussions about hymns and worship material recommended for the new hymnal. Perhaps no other hymnal in the history of the church has received such painstaking scrutiny and deliberation.

In the Methodist tradition (the E.U.B. tradition is somewhat different) "official" hymnals are those authorized by the General Conference, the denomination's official legislative body which meets every four years. For much of the church's history, the hymnal was also given official imprimatur by being signed by the bishops. Other hymnals might be published and used in the churches, but only the "official" hymnal was approved.

When the Methodist and Evangelical United Brethren

denominations merged in 1968, it was evident that a common hymnal was needed to represent the united church. This did not seem appropriate immediately after merger, however, since both the E.U.B. hymnal of 1955 and the Methodist hymnal of 1966 were just being accepted by the churches and would be serviceable for some time.

The late 1970s, however, brought more and more talk about moving ahead with a "United" Methodist hymnal. The strongest agitation for this came not from those seeking a symbol of a consummated merger, but from growing feminist sentiment. The "inclusive language" issue was surfacing, and the hymnal, according to some, represented the church's "sexist" bias.

The call for a new hymnal came primarily from seminaries and church boards and agencies. In the early 1970s, concern about sexist language was directed mostly toward the generic use of the word "man." Many people argued that the continual use of the word "man" to describe all people seemed to exclude women. Why refer to the head of a committee as "chairman" when that person is a woman? Why use the phrase "Christ died for all mankind" when we believe Christ died for both women and men?

But soon the idea of inclusive language was expanded to call into question gender-specific language about God. If God is a Spirit, then God is neither male nor female. To use only male-oriented words to refer to God demeans women (or so the argument went). Therefore, continual references to God as "he," "Father," "King" or even "Lord" ought to be avoided or, if not discontinued completely, balanced with feminine-type metaphors.

Inclusive language soon became a cause, and the seminaries and church boards and agencies, ever susceptible to causes (at least liberal ones) became the primary agitators for change. Many seminaries developed language guidelines for classroom and chapel use. Some went further and developed policies which not only encouraged inclusive language but also punished any detractors by marking down their grades for non-cooperation.

Going even further, church publications like *Response* and *New World Outlook* purged all copy that referred to God as "Father" or "he." Church school publications were somewhat more tempered in the extent to which they bought into the inclusive language agenda, but they, too, were affected.

Meanwhile, the concept of inclusive language was expanding still further. Perhaps other groups besides women felt demeaned by language. Negative references to "darkness" could be degrading to blacks. References to "heathen lands" could be insulting to developing nations. The use of words like "dumb" could be offensive to deaf persons. It was even argued that a phrase like "being seated at the right hand" was demeaning to left-handed persons.

For many people these were not incidental matters. They were of the essence. A church that persisted in using language that was sexist, racist, nationalistic, militaristic, imperialistic or handicappistic had lost its way and was, in the minds of some, guilty of heresy as heinous as any heresies of the past.

The hymnal seemed the last barrier preventing a more inclusive church. A new hymnal that would drop inappropriate hymns, include new hymns with inclusive-type images and change words and phrases to fit the new understanding of inclusiveness was needed.

The argument was lost, however, on most United Methodists, who found it hard to understand why references to God as Father should offend women. If, after all, Jesus called God "Father," why is it inappropriate for people today to do so? Others argued that modifying the language and images of hymns would be modifying the language and images of Scripture, since hymn texts are often drawn from Scripture. Still others noted that language that is purged of gender-linked images and pronouns loses much poetic richness, becoming a bland language more like technical, ideological jargon than the language of faith. Large numbers of ordinary Christians felt that criticism of the language they used was criticism of them as persons and of their faith.

With United Methodists holding these conflicting views, it is no wonder that the 1980 General Conference passed two seemingly contradictory resolutions regarding the hymnal within a ten-minute period. One was to remove the word "hymnody" from a four-year study on God language and inclusiveness. The other was to ask the Board of Discipleship to be attentive to inclusive language in relation to persons and to God in the preliminary study on the new hymnal.

Many people argued the importance of the hymnal in the life of the church—that it was United Methodists' catechism, their

Book of Common Prayer—and ought, therefore, to be a unifying force. Others, however, were so distraught by the language controversies already embroiling the church that they were ready to vote for no new hymnal rather than a new hymnal that would be divisive.

And the inclusive language issue was only one of a number of controversies surrounding the idea of a new United Methodist hymnal. Some argued that in a time when the church was interested in peace, we were sending the wrong message by including so many hymns that spoke of "battles," "soldiers" and "weapons" (the charge of militarism). And should we include patriotic hymns which seem to glorify our country at the expense of other nations, suggesting that God loves America more than other lands?

Added to these issues were concerns relating to ethnic heritage. Almost all of the hymns in the hymnal reflected the white, English-speaking, somewhat pretentious preferences of former hymnal committees. In a church interested in reaching out to people of other nations, races and traditions, ought not the hymnal reflect the music of those cultures? This seemed especially true for Negro spirituals and black gospel, which had been an important part of American Methodism from its beginning (see chapter nine).

Any new hymnal would also grapple with theological matters. How would the hymnal handle traditional evangelical doctrines such as Original Sin, the Substitutionary Atonement, Salvation, Judgment and the Second Coming? Recent hymnals, reflecting the liberalism of the seminaries, had been much less affirming of hymns that stressed those doctrines. Would the new hymnal continue that trend?

And, not the least concern by any means, were matters of style and taste. Highbrow or lowbrow? German chorales or country-western gospel? Would the new hymnal be open to Scripture choruses? Contemporary gospel?

Someone commented that work on a new hymnal could not have come at a worse time. The United Methodist Church in the 1980s seemed to be floundering, rent apart by special interest groups and uncertainty about its mission in the world. The same 1984 General Conference that authorized a hymnal committee also created a theological study task force and a task force to study the mission of the church. These actions seemed designed not to proclaim the faith and carry out Christ's mission, but to determine if there were a faith to proclaim and a mission to carry out. As for the hymnal, several people commented that perhaps the best action would be to publish a number of special hymnals, offering a variety of options since it seemed obvious that the new hymnal could not win. It would probably offend everyone.

The fears of the critics, however, did not (at least for the time being) materialize. The hymnal was finally approved by the 1988 General Conference amid genuine rejoicing. It seemed to have found a middle way on the language issue, in which language about people was rendered inclusive but traditional language about God in traditional hymns was respected. The evangelical legacy (gospel hymns) was included to an extent unknown in previous Methodist hymnals. The black heritage was finally recognized in an official hymnal, and there was a smattering of hymns from a number of different cultural traditions. The new hymnal included some Scripture choruses, some hymns stressing peace with justice and some hymns with fresh, contemporary images based on scriptural themes. Editor Carlton Young called it a "populist" hymnal, meaning the committee often based decisions on the research about what hymns people wanted, rather than on what the committee itself preferred.

To Do

Following are some very different kinds of hymns. Discuss their appropriateness for your church setting by answering the following questions:

1. Is the hymn known, or could it be easily learned?
2. Are the hymn's images and language faithful to biblical teaching?
3. Is the message appropriate for your church's needs?
4. What does the hymn say?
5. Does this hymn speak to a particular group that is a part of your United Methodist church?
6. Does the hymn have special meaning for you?
7. Do you know of people for whom it has special meaning?

"Rise Up, O Men of God" (UMH #576)
"God of the Sparrow, God of the Whale" (UMH #122)
"I Heard an Old, Old Story" (UMH #370)

"A Mighty Fortress Is Our God" (UMH #110)
"See the Morning Sun Ascending" (UMH #674)
"America"(UMH #697)
"De Tierra Lejana Venimos" (UMH #243)
"El Shaddai" (UMH #123)

Two

How Hymns Function

My wife, Ruth, and I were discussing favorite hymns in a group. The leader asked, "What hymn is particularly special to you?" It was Ruth's turn to answer, and before she spoke I knew what she would say: "Yes, there is a hymn."

Great is thy faithfulness, O God my Father;
there is no shadow of turning with thee. (UMH #140)

It was the same hymn I would have mentioned.

I was a freshman at Taylor University, where I sang in the university chorale. Our director, Professor Pearson, like all trained musicians, wanted to sing "good" music. We were, after all, a college choir. It did not seem appropriate for college choirs to sing choruses and Sunday school songs. We needed to sing Bach, Vaughn Williams and masses written in Latin.

But the choir members—at least some—wanted to sing more contemporary or lively or at least familiar music. We saw concerts not as performances but as opportunities for witness. We wanted gospel songs and spirituals.

So we struck a compromise. Each concert included a section named "Hymns" toward the end, during which the choir sang several hymns—not anthems, not hymn arrangements, but hymns—right out of the book. Those hymns, and particularly one hymn, stick in my memory:

all I have needed thy hand hath provided;
great is thy faithfulness, Lord, unto me!

I associate those words with churches: city churches, country churches, Methodist churches, Baptist churches and with people in whose homes choir members stayed—a couple on a farm in Minnesota, a young family in Iowa. I also associate those words with a time in my life when the Lord was revealing all kinds of new things about who he is, and that he might have a plan for me.

One night, as I recall, we sang that hymn in the bus coming back to school from Cincinnati.

Pardon for sin and a peace that endureth,
thine own dear presence to cheer and to guide.

I asked some friends if they would like to go to the prayer chapel with me when we got back to school. They did, and sometime in the early morning hours I prayed a prayer of submission and asked for an infilling of the Holy Spirit.

strength for today and bright hope for tomorrow,
blessings all mine, with ten thousand beside!

A year later the choir was still singing Latin chorales and contemporary anthems and a few favorite hymns, including a carry-over from the year before.

summer and winter and springtime and harvest,
sun, moon, and stars in their courses above
join with all nature in manifold witness
to thy great faithfulness, mercy, and love.

That year I was falling in love with a girl who shared the long rehearsals, the bus trips and the conversations about matters of life and God's Spirit. We both came to appreciate the Bach chorales, but we also agreed that the hymns were what really moved the people who came to the concerts.

thou changest not, thy compassions, they fail not;
as thou hast been thou forever wilt be.

Somehow in the linking together of mind and spirit and music, a line of that hymn conjures up memories: an inner city church in Philadelphia on Easter, a country church in Maryland, a broom closet of a magnificent old church. Laughter, jokes, eating on the choir bus. Our choir did not have to be rehearsing or in concert to sing. We sang around tables, in the hotel lobby, on the bus. The songs became prayers and testimonies and part of a common life.

great is thy faithfulness, Lord, unto me!

Years later we returned to that campus with our daughter. It must always be a difficult time for parents when their first child leaves home. The children's books, teddy bears and high school pom-poms are on the shelf. The conflicts over who was dated and how late the dates lasted and what might have gone on that we didn't know about had left some twinges of anxiety. We had prayed about schools and God's will and that our daughter would meet the right friends and find right answers to difficult questions. It was a proud moment, but we were not overly confident parents and needed a reassuring word.

We did not anticipate it would come so dramatically. We moved to the chapel for parents' orientation. Whatever was said on that occasion has long since been forgotten, but it does not matter. What we remember is the opening hymn, sung before anything else was said.

> *Great is thy faithfulness, O God my Father;*
> *there is no shadow of turning with thee;*
> *thou changest not, thy compassions, they fail not;*
> *as thou hast been thou forever wilt be.*

We both wept.

There is a reason why certain hymns become our favorites. It has to do with memory, with people we have known and places we have been. These images, feelings and experiences are related somehow in the mystery of the human soul to text and music. Sometimes this relationship is so deeply ingrained within us we cannot explain, or may not even know, the connections. But the connections are there, whether the music is secular or sacred. Music speaks about who we are, where we come from, our philosophy of life, the people we belong to and, for believers, who God is, and how he has spoken.

If I were to list the great hymns of the church I would not include "Great Is Thy Faithfulness." The tune is not particularly memorable. The poetry of the text is not exceptional. But it is still one of my favorite hymns because of the way it functions: It connects me with past images and experiences and evokes a sense of God's faithfulness.

In one sense, a discussion of hymns is a discussion of faith and a faith language.

Believers operate in several worlds. One is the world of sight, sense and smell, the everyday work world which we share with school teachers and bus drivers and the neighbors across the street. In this world we talk about whether it will rain and will the Cubs win and what happened to the price of corn. This is the world of politicians and *People* magazine and Pontiacs. It is the secular world, and in it we use secular, MacGraw-Hill language suitable for classrooms, department stores and television newscasts.

But believers also live in a world of faith, which in an important sense is more real than the other world. In this world we speak of angels and old rugged crosses and a heavenly Father. We refer to things that really matter—how we were created, how our forebears in the faith crossed the Red Sea, how we are saved by grace.

Sometimes even Christians have difficulty expressing themselves in this spiritual world. Prayer and worship language do not come easily for us who spend so many hours in that other world. But at certain points in our lives we connect with the spiritual world. In devotional study and in the freedom that comes when music combines with belief, we meet and worship together as people of faith.

This is true not only for individuals, but also for families, churches, ethnic groups and denominations. Because we have a shared history and similar spiritual experiences, we are connected with the covenant people of God. Within the family of believers there are differences in nationality, ethnicity, geographical region and differences that result from varied experiences. But at the same time we share a common Christ.

Some years ago the retired president of Asbury Theological Seminary, Dr. J.C. McPheeters, suffered a stroke. The stroke so impaired him physically that he was unable to speak, though his friends and family were sure he could hear and understand when he was spoken to. One day a friend visited Dr. McPheeters in the hospital, and during the course of the visit started to sing, "Amazing Grace." As he did so, a most unusual thing happened. The venerable seminary president joined in, and the two sang together. It seemed a miracle, perhaps an instant cure, but it was not. When the song was over, the victim still could not speak, no matter how he tried. So it was in the following months. The saint of God could not speak, but he could sing the hymns of faith.

> *'Twas grace that taught my heart to fear,*
> *and grace my fears relieved;*
> *how precious did that grace appear,*
> *the hour I first believed. (UMH #378)*

This incident may illustrate some medical fact—that one portion of the brain may be affected by a stroke while another part remains relatively unaffected. But it also illustrates a spiritual truth—music influences us in a way that defies rational explanation. It touches the spirit, and God works through music to abide in us with his Spirit.

This is the reason we want to sing the same hymns over and over even though we would object to hearing the same sermon repeated frequently. We ask our pastors to prepare new, creative messages, but we often resist the introduction of new, creative hymns.

This is not necessarily bad, because hymns serve a different purpose than sermons. They have a different kind of power.

Because of our love for certain time-tested hymns, any study which proposes to explore who United Methodists are as a people must not look primarily at the new hymns (there are plenty of those in the hymnal) but at old hymns—the hymns of the Wesleys, of camp meetings, of congregational praise and church conferences. An important questions to ask is, "How have these hymns functioned in our lives?" We could try to understand United Methodism through statistical study—how many blacks, whites, people over sixty-five and under twenty, liberals and conservatives the church contains. We could analyze who the bishops are and what our Sunday school literature is like and how United Methodists feel about nuclear disarmament or smoking cigarettes. But we might also understand United Methodists by discovering why "O For a Thousand Tongues to Sing" is number one in the hymnal and why "How Great Thou Art" presently ranks as the favorite United

Methodist hymn and why we have so many hymns about Christmas.

Let us pursue our investigation of United Methodism by discussing how several different hymns function for at least some in the church.

O Come, All Ye Faithful (UMH #234)

This is truly an ecumenical hymn. Baptists, Roman Catholics and Nazarenes, as well as United Methodists, sing it. The refrain is sometimes used as a charismatic chorus. It is sung in English, Latin and African dialects and in numerous other languages around the world. The hymn means Christmas and everything that goes with it, from family gatherings to Sunday school programs to candlelight communion services. Its use is so widespread that it has become part of general American culture. During the Christmas season it can be heard in department stores, on television or radio (sung by non-Christian entertainers) and at office parties. It can be sung in public school Christmas programs that usually, because secular education bans anything religious, presents Christmas in terms of Santa Claus and reindeer.

This is an example of a hymn that transcends denominations, ethnic groups and theological persuasions and appeals to a large part of secular society. It suggests to us the mystery of God's gift in Jesus Christ and reminds us of experiences we associate with Christmas: family gatherings, Sunday school programs, caroling and gift giving.

Children of the Heavenly Father (UMH #141)

In contrast to "O Come, All Ye Faithful," "Children of the Heavenly Father" is an ethnic hymn loved by Scandinavians and particularly by people of Swedish background. When the hymnal committee discussed this hymn, someone asked, "Who sings this?" The answer was, "People from Minnesota." People of Scandinavian descent are concentrated in Minnesota, and they sing this hymn whether they are in Lutheran or Baptist or United Methodist churches.

I once attended a concert given by a Baptist choir from Sweden in a Swedish Baptist (General Conference) church in St. Paul. The highlight of the concert was the hymn sung in Swedish.

Children of the heavenly Father
safely in his bosom gather;
nestling bird nor star in heaven
such a refuge e' er was given.

Young and old alike wept openly. I don't know all the images that hymn brought to mind that day (sometimes we don't understand such things even within ourselves), but for that congregation this hymn touched something having to do with home, family, a loving heavenly Father and the past. For many Lutherans the hymn functions as both a baptism and a funeral hymn. While the hymn is really about God's greater family, it has been properly classified as related to the Christian home.

Onward, Christian Soldiers (UMH #575)

If the committee that prepared the 1989 hymnal is remembered for one thing, perhaps it will be the flap over "Onward Christian Soldiers." One reason the controversy occurred was because a number of people failed to appreciate how a hymn like "Onward Christian Soldiers" functions.

The argument for removing the hymn goes something like this: Our society is deeply involved in the sin of "militarism," a way of thinking and acting that relies on military power, bombs and guns to settle differences between nations. In contrast, the Scriptures call on us to be peacemakers, to reject war and its weapons as a means of maintaining our nation's security.

Hymns that speak of "war" and "foes" and "battles" encourage, whether consciously or unconsciously, our involvement in militaristic thoughts and actions. Those hymns, the argument continues, ought either to be softened or replaced with hymns that speak of peace and justice and love.

Indeed, some music *is* martial in character, very nationalistic in its message and intended to arouse patriotic and militaristic fervor. But only a poor reading of who United Methodists are and how popular hymns function could link "Onward Christian Soldiers" with that kind of "militarism."

"Onward Christian Soldiers" was written for a children's festival, and for many it still functions as a children's song. As one person said, "If we remove 'Onward Christian Soldiers' from the hymnal, what will Bible school children use to march to class?"

On another level, the hymn often functions as a call to action—we are Christians and ought to be doing something to make plain the cause of Christ. The warfare is spiritual, but we fight the forces of disunity, apathy and unconcern as well as Satan.

The nation naturally reacted negatively to a hymnal committee that sought to impose an interpretation of "Onward Christian Soldiers" that was foreign to the great majority of United Methodists. It simply is not true that most people transfer the meaning of hymns and faith language into social and political issues of the day. Traditionally pacifist churches such as Quakers, Brethren and Mennonites sing "Onward Christian Soldiers" as lustily as cadets at West Point. The great evangelist Dwight L. Moody (who was a pacifist) would not sing the song, not because of the war imagery, but because Christian people he knew were not dedicated enough to be called soldiers in their battle against sin.

By letter count, the score was twelve thousand who wrote to the committee objecting to the suggestion that the hymn be removed because it is "militaristic," to twenty-four who supported the removal.

Curiously, the committee's action might have introduced a new function for the hymn. Since the much-publicized discussion of "Onward Christian Soldiers," the hymn is actually becoming known as a patriotic hymn to be sung on Memorial Day or the Fourth of July.

Lift Every Voice and Sing (UMH #519)

Certain songs unite a people's hopes and aspirations, such as patriotic songs or national anthems. "O Beautiful for Spacious Skies" is an example of a song primarily intended to express love for America, and only secondarily meant to be a Christian hymn of praise (for that reason some persons object to using it in a service of Christian worship).

"Lift Every Voice and Sing" functions in a similar manner. It is known as the "Black National Anthem." As a song it was intended to express the black struggle for freedom in America, while at the same time conveying thanks to God and pledging loyalty to country. The team of brothers who wrote and composed it, James Weldon and John Rosamond Johnson, were more involved in show business than Christian music.

Nevertheless, the song is usually sung gospel style and very often is an expression of faith. It exemplifies the way the distinction between secular and sacred music is often blurred in the black tradition.

When sung by people outside the black tradition, the song becomes a means of identification with the faith and hopes of the black community.

How Great Thou Art (UMH #77)

How does a hymn become a favorite? "How Great Thou Art" is not an easy song for congregations to sing. However, it has become closely identified with evangelical faith in the latter half of the twentieth century, probably because of its familiarity and its message.

There is no question that its familiarity comes from association with Billy Graham, the most popular contemporary evangelist, and his soloist, George Beverly Shea. The song's message links the wonder of creation, the wonder of the atonement and the wonder of the Second Coming and eternal life.

The song also reminds us of the tremendous influence nationally known Christian leaders have upon our faith. "How Great Thou Art" was an obscure Swedish gospel hymn dating back from the nineteenth century until it became a trademark of George Beverly Shea and the Billy Graham evangelistic crusades.

It is not the first hymn to become identified with a specific evangelist and his music leader. "In the Garden" and "He Lives" were trademarks of the Billy Sunday and Homer Rodeheaver crusades. Similarly, Dwight L. Moody and his song evangelist Ira Sankey popularized "What a Friend We Have in Jesus" and "I Love to Tell the Story."

Such crusades have become signs of renewed evangelical faith at times when increasingly secular forces in society seem to be eroding such faith. In the case of "How Great Thou Art," those who identified with the work of Billy Graham became attached to the song. Those who were less enthusiastic about Billy Graham were less attached to the song. The high regard of common, ordinary United Methodists for the hymn indicates that evangelical faith that best characterizes United Methodists.

To Do

Have each member of the group or class identify a favorite hymn and answer the following questions:

1. Do you associate a person or a group of persons with the hymn?

2. Do you associate the hymn with a certain place?

3. Do you associate an experience with the hymn?

Three

O for a
Thousand
Tongues to Sing

O for a thousand tongues to sing
my great Redeemer's praise!
The glories of my God and King,
the triumphs of his grace! (UMH #57)

If one hymn can rightfully claim the title of "The Methodist National Anthem," it is "O for a Thousand Tongues to Sing." This hymn has traditionally been number one in Methodist hymnals.

The hymn as originally written by Charles Wesley had eighteen verses. In the interest of brevity (it is possible to have too much of even a good thing), recent hymnals have carried only six verses. However, because of the importance of the hymn and its message, the new 1989 hymnal contains nearly all of the original verses. To spend time with the hymn—the message, the mood, the spirit, the joy—is to sense the story of United Methodism. To sing it with heart-felt faith is to worship the living God and testify to the heritage United Methodists hold as precious.

My gracious Master and my God,
assist me to proclaim,
to spread through all the earth abroad
the honors of thy name. (v. 8)

"O for a Thousand Tongues to Sing" was written in May 1739 and was originally entitled, "For the Anniversary Day of One's Conversion." A year before, in May 1738, both John and Charles Wesley had come by faith to a living relationship with Jesus Christ.

For John the conversion was dramatic. After a strict religious upbringing, a very disciplined devotional life, ordination as a priest in the Church of England and a trip to America to attempt to save the Indians, John Wesley came to the realization that he did not have the faith he preached about. A Moravian friend, Peter Bohler, helped him understand that salvation depends on the merits of Christ alone. It is not by works but by faith that we come to know Christ.

On May 24, 1738, while attending a small group in a room off Aldersgate Street in London, John Wesley felt his heart "strangely warmed." Jesus Christ came into his life in a new way, bringing the assurance of salvation.

On this glad day the glorious Sun
of Righteousness arose,
on my benighted soul he shone,
and filled it with repose. (v. 2)

John's description of what happened is found in his journal for May 24, 1738: "I felt I did trust in Christ, Christ alone for salvation, and an assurance was given me. He had taken away my sins, even mine, and saved me from the law of sin and death."

Sudden expired the legal strife,
'twas then I ceased to grieve,
my second, real, living life
I then began to live. (v. 3)

The conversion of Charles Wesley, though not as dramatic, was no less real. Charles had the same strict religious upbringing, had joined the strictly disciplined "Holy Club" that John belonged to, had also been ordained a priest in the Church of England and gone to America as a missionary. Like John, Charles came first to a commitment to the doctrine of salvation by faith. He writes in his Journal for Wednesday, May 17, 1738,

Who would believe our church had been founded on this important article of justification by faith alone? I am astonished I should ever think this a new doctrine; especially while our Articles and Homilies stand unrepealed. . . . From this time I endeavoured to ground as many of our friends as came in this fundamental truth, salvation by faith alone.

A few days later Charles came to living faith.

Then with my heart I first believed,
believed with faith divine,
power with the Holy Ghost received
to call the Savior mine. (v. 4)

In the year following May 1738, the Methodist revival, birthed in the conversion of John and Charles Wesley, began to spread. The Wesleys proclaimed an evangelical message centering on Jesus Christ.

Jesus! the name that charms our fears,
that bids our sorrows cease;
'tis music in the sinner's ears,
'tis life, and health, and peace! (v. 9)

This Christ-centered message contrasted with the deism and rationalism which had crept into the religious thinking of much of eighteenth-century England. Today we would call Methodist preaching "evangelical." It refuted a religion which stressed the sacraments and being rightly related to the church (sacramentalism) by focusing on the Reformation doctrine of salvation by faith alone.

Look unto him, ye nations, own
your God, ye fallen race!
Look, and be saved, through faith alone,
be justified by grace! (v. 13)

In contrast to forms of Protestant Scholasticism which lifted up creeds and right beliefs as the essence of the faith (confessionalism), Methodism's evangelical message stressed a new birth that can be experienced personally.

I felt my Lord's atoning blood
close to my soul applied;
me, me he loved—the Son of God

for me, for me he died! (v. 5)

In contrast to the cold, dead religion that characterized the church of that day, the Methodist message was full of power and joy.

> *Hear him, ye deaf, his praise, ye dumb,*
> *your loosened tongues employ;*
> *ye blind, behold your Savior come,*
> *and leap, ye lame, for joy. (v. 12)*

To a great extent, the Methodist movement defined the word "evangelical." It was an understanding of Christianity centering on the person and work of Jesus Christ, particularly (in the words of the Abingdon Catechism) his "incarnate life, atoning death, and glorious resurrection." But it was more than an "understanding." It was a message preached and lived: salvation by faith, the new birth, holy living and a desire to reach the lost.

> *He breaks the power of canceled sin,*
> *he sets the prisoner free;*
> *his blood can make the foulest clean;*
> *his blood availed for me. (v. 10)*

Whenever possible, Wesley preached about salvation in the established churches of England, but since the message was controversial (as the preaching of the gospel often is), invitations to preach were often withdrawn. When the opportunity to speak in churches was denied, John Wesley joined his friend George Whitefield to preach in the open air.

It was in the open air, among miners and poor, common people, that the revival took hold and began to spread across England. The journals of both John and Charles are filled with accounts of dozens and even hundreds of persons crying to God for mercy. John Wesley had the gift of administration as well as power in preaching and was able to organize the converts who came to him every day into small groups called societies. The societies prayed together, encouraged each other and studied together.

They also sang. The hymns of Isaac Watts and the Moravians were favorites at first, but very soon the societies also began to sing hymns composed by Charles. These hymns were directly related to the preaching and teaching of the early Methodists. "O for a Thousand Tongues to Sing" was based on a remark by the Wesleys' friend, Peter Bohler, who commented one day, "If I had a thousand tongues I'd praise Christ with them all."

But more than the remark by Bohler, the hymn was a reflection, one year later, of the conversion of the Wesleys. As it was sung, many Methodists used it to reflect on their own conversions. Methodism had not come about because of doctrinal controversy, political intrigue or personality differences. It grew out of a revival, and the singing, especially hymns of the Wesleys, was often the testimonies, teachings and even the altar calls of that revival.

> *See all your sins on Jesus laid;*
> *the Lamb of God was slain,*
> *his soul was once an offering made*
> *for every soul of man. (v. 14)*

Wesley Hymns in Perspective

How did the Wesleys' music relate to the larger renewal of hymn-singing and evangelical faith in eighteenth-century England? To answer this question, let us think about Great Britain (and America) in the early 1700s. Though hymns and hymn singing in some form had been a part of Christian worship since New Testament times, in the English-speaking world hymns had become dull and tradition-bound. Christian congregations, both Catholic and Protestant, did not sing often, or well. The available music was primarily German chorales or Calvinist metrical Psalms. Few hymn writers dared to venture much beyond the literal words of Scripture.

Isaac Watts, sometimes called the Father of the English Hymn, preceded the Wesleys by only a few years. He brought new life to dissenting churches (primarily Congregationalist and Baptist) by introducing hymns which interpreted the Psalms in the light of New Testament truth about Jesus. Thus Psalm 72:1, 5:

> *Endow the king with your justice, O God, . . .*
> *He will endure as long as the sun, . . .*

became, when written as a hymn,

> *Jesus shall reign where'er the sun*
> *does its successive journeys run. (UMH #157)*

To sing only verbatim Old Testament words, Watts argued, was to throw the "veil of Moses" over the hearts of the people. Under Watts' pen the words of Psalm 98:4, 6, 9:

Shout for joy to the Lord, all the earth, . . .
shout for joy before the Lord, the King. . . .
for he comes to judge the earth.

became the well-known Christmas hymn extolling Jesus Christ,

Joy to the world! the Lord is come.
Let earth receive her King. (UMH #246)

But Isaac Watts did not stop with the Psalms. Soon other scriptural passages, and then all of life, began to be reflected in his hymns.

When I survey the wondrous cross
on which the Prince of Glory died,
my richest gain I count but loss,
_and pour contempt on all my pride. (UMH #298)

The hymns of Watts revived hymn singing in England and America. In the American colonies they became a vital force in what is often called the First Great Awakening, the revival in New England in the 1730s associated with persons like Jonathan Edwards and George Whitefield.

The Wesleys learned a great deal from Watts and also from their friends the Moravians (who wrote primarily in German). But their hymns went even further. Watts and dissenting evangelicals had cracked the church door to admit the fresh air of evangelical singing, and the Methodists threw the door wide open.

For Methodists, singing was no longer an appendage to worship, reserved for festivals and other special occasions. It was an integral part of life and not restricted to formal worship in church buildings. One could sing with friends in small groups or alone while harvesting in the field or walking to town. The hymn texts were paired with singable and sometimes popular tunes. As a result, song linked the gospel to popular culture and became an important ingredient in the Methodist revival that swept England.

The genius of this Methodist music is illustrated by a further look at "O for a Thousand Tongues to Sing." To appreciate any hymn, it is helpful to ask certain questions: 1. What is the hymn really about? 2. Who is speaking? 3. Who is being addressed?

What Is the Hymn About?

In our churches we often use "O for a Thousand Tongues to Sing" as an opening hymn of praise in worship, and so it was meant to be. But the hymn is much more than a general praising of God for his goodness to us and for the world about us. It is specific thanks to Jesus Christ for what he accomplished on the cross and for the new life in Christ available to believers. This thanksgiving is followed by an emotional, compassionate appeal to the unsaved to believe in Jesus Christ. To explain it another way, this song is about the gospel.

Who Is Speaking?

This may seem like a strange question. We are tempted to answer that, obviously, church attenders are speaking (or singing). For Wesley, however, church attenders were seekers at a point somewhere on their Christian journey. They might, as in the following hymn, assume the place of a lost sinner crying for mercy:

> *Depth of mercy! Can there be*
> *mercy still reserved for me? (UMH #355)*

Hymn #387 represents the testimony of the believer at the moment of salvation:

> *'Tis Love! 'tis Love! thou diedst for me.*
> *I hear thy whisper in my heart.*
> *The morning breaks, the shadows flee,*
> *pure, Universal Love thou art. (v. 9)*

The believer in pain and distress could sing hymn #479:

> *Jesus, lover of my soul, let me to thy bosom fly,*
> *while the nearer waters roll,*
> *while the tempest still is high.*

The congregation joins the believer seeking Christian Perfection (sanctification) in hymn #410:

> *I want a principle within*
> *of watchful, godly fear.*

In "O for a Thousand Tongues to Sing," we celebrate as a congregation the new-found joy of salvation (the hymn was originally titled, "For the Anniversary Day of One's Conversion"). However, even when singing (or reflecting, since seldom are all verses sung) from the vantage point of a recent convert, we follow the new believer's testimony through the stages to salvation.

These stages correspond roughly to what we might call "Five Spiritual Laws." They are: sin (v. 2), justification (v. 3), free grace (v. 4), assurance (v. 5) and regeneration (v. 5).

The new 1989 hymnal seeks to reflect the spiritual insight of the Wesley hymns in the order of salvation (or points along the spiritual journey) by organizing the hymns in "The Power of the Holy Spirit" section in a somewhat similar fashion.The section identifies three kinds of grace found in United Methodist thinking: prevenient grace (grace that God gives us even before we are Christians—sometimes linked with "free will"); justifying grace (grace by which we are carried from darkness to light and "saved"); and sanctifying grace (grace which enables us to live holy lives).

Under the various kinds of grace (see the hymnal's table of contents) are subsections which we might call stages in the journey of faith:
* invitation (to the sinner to believe)
* repentance
* pardon
* assurance
* rebirth and the new creature
* personal holiness
* social holiness
* prayer, trust and hope
* strength in tribulation.

The depth and power of Wesley hymns contrast sharply with many contemporary hymns, both gospel and otherwise. Much gospel music tends to be either "preachy" (what's wrong with the world), or stuck on one point in the "order of salvation," stressing how wonderful it is to be a Christian. Liberal, or mainline, contemporary religious music tends to ask God to help us do better and makes no distinctions between being saved and lost.

Who Is Being Addressed?
The answer is (of course) that God is being addressed in "O

for a Thousand Tongues to Sing." But this is not just God-in-general as in many liberal hymns (see chapter seven). In Wesley hymns, this is always the God who is at some point along the path of the great story of salvation.

In hymn #287 the soul (or "self") speaks in the presence of Jesus on the cross:

O Love divine, what hast thou done!
Th' immortal God hath died for me!

Hymn #240, a cry of joy to the world, describes angels singing in the presence of the Christ in the manger:

Hark! the herald angels sing,
"Glory to the newborn King."

Hymn #302 is spoken in the presence of the risen Christ of Easter:

Christ the Lord is risen today . . .

But not all the Wesley hymns (or other hymns) are addressed to God, or assume the immediate presence of God. Some hymns are addressed to the church, as hymn #513:

Soldiers of Christ, arise,
and put your armor on.

This is not unusual. Many hymns are addressed to the church or to the worshiping community. Wesley hymns, however, introduce an additional feature not found in other hymns of the day: Verses are addressed to sinners, outside the saving grace of Christ.

These hymns have the amazing quality of being able to express the compassionate, broken heart without sounding judgmental. In doing so, they introduced to the evangelical world the "invitation hymn," along with two of the most precious words in evangelical faith: "come" and "home." Hymn #342, verse 5, is an example:

Come, O my guilty brethren, come,
groaning beneath your load of sin;
his bleeding heart shall make you room,
his open side shall take you in.
He calls you now, invites you home:
come, O my guilty brethren, come.

Methodist societies sang this invitation across the fields and in the homes of eighteenth-century England. It is not difficult to see why there was revival.

With this understanding of the question, "Who Is Being Addressed?" we find several audiences in "O for a Thousand Tongues to Sing." They are,

- the Triune God addressed in praise (vv. 1, 7);
- the testimony of salvation addressed to the congregation (or the world) (v. 2);
- Jesus addressed in petition (v. 8);
- the gospel message addressed to the congregation (or the world) (vv. 9-11);
- those outside the gospel invited to believe (vv. 12-17). These include:

    a) the spiritually deaf, blind and lame (v. 12)

    b) the nations (vv. 13-14)

    c) harlots, publicans and thieves (v. 15)

    d) murderers and sons of lust and pride (v. 16).

Charles Wesley wrote approximately eight thousand hymns. The earliest Methodist hymnals carried up to five hundred of these hymns, many of which were (and are) devotional gems. Those early hymnals were one of God's most powerful tools used to bring about England's great revival in the eighteenth century and America's great revival in the nineteenth century.

To Do

Answer these questions about the following Charles Wesley hymns:

1. What is the hymn really about?
2. Who is speaking?
3. Who is being addressed?

"O Love Divine, What Hast Thou Done?"(UMH #287)

"Sinners, Turn: Why Will You Die?" (UMH #346)

"Depth of Mercy! Can There Be" (UMH #355)

"Blow Ye the Trumpet, Blow" (UMH #379)

"Jesus, Thine All-Victorious Love"(UMH #422)

"Come, Holy Ghost, Our Hearts Inspire" (UMH #603)

"O Thou Who This Mysterious Bread" (UMH #613)

Four

Methodist Music

As I recall, the first question I was asked years ago by the Conference Board of Ministerial Training and Qualifications in preparation for ordination was, "How do you feel about the Methodist hymnal?"

The question was not a surprise. A few weeks earlier I had completed a seminary course on music and worship. I had been indoctrinated to know the difference between good music and bad, between good and bad theology in hymns and between what was and what was not acceptable in Methodist worship.

The so-called "gospel hymns" did not fare well in the class, whether we were discussing music or theology or any other basis for judgment. "Pass Me Not, O Gentle Savior" (UMH #351), according to the professor, "could not be defended on any grounds." "Thou, My Everlasting Portion" (UMH #407) was much too repetitive. "Blessed Assurance" (UMH #369) called attention to itself. "Softly and Tenderly Jesus Is Calling" (UMH #348) didn't say anything. "There Is a Fountain Filled with Blood" (UMH #622) was bad theology and abominable imagery.

The class learned that pastors had a responsibility to teach congregations "good music." Despite what people loved and preferred, they "deserved" to be led to something better. Gospel music, with its continual references to "pie in the sky," subjective experience, emphasis on blood and repetitive texts and tunes, represented much of what was wrong with the church. It led to extremes, such as "Put Your Snout Under the Spout Where the Gospel Comes Out" and "Ain't No Flies on My Jesus."

Fortunately—so the class was told—the church would not have to bear with it much longer because, like much that was frivolous, this kind of music and the religion it represented was passing from the scene. An advancing culture simply would not tolerate it. Could any of us imagine respectable people who had "come of age" singing such "trash" as "Standing, standing, standing on the promises of God" (UMH #374)?

Later, on further reflection, some of us were uneasy about what had happened in class. We knew a lot of people, modern and otherwise, who enjoyed singing "Standing on the Promises." We felt that to ridicule the music was to ridicule the faith behind the music and the people who held that faith.

Still, the course prepared me for what the leaders in the church considered acceptable "Methodist music." It was the music from the hymnal most often sung in Methodist churches with organs. It was "For the Beauty of the Earth," "Holy, Holy, Holy" and "This Is My Father's World." The other music—which could be found in the paperback "unofficial" songbooks—was suspect. It belonged to people of the hills, Baptists in the South, or the tabernacles located in the poor part of town.

How did I feel about the Methodist hymnal? "It was fine," I told the members of the Board. While it was not the hymnal used in the churches I served, it was the hymnal in my home church and the one I had grown up with. One of the board members patiently counseled me on the importance of making sure our churches used the "official" hymnal.

Later, one of the older members of the conference counseled me a bit further, explaining that the churches I was serving, though it was certainly not my fault, were "not really Methodist churches." Their spirit, attitude and beliefs seemed more, he thought, like Nazarene churches or "some group like that."

I am glad the people of the Geneva Circuit did not hear this opinion. They were firmly convinced they were Methodist churches. They worshiped and believed the same way their Methodist fathers and mothers had. The Union Chapel church held Methodist "class meetings," had sent six young men into the Methodist ministry and set their goal for world service twice as high as the asking because they believed it was money for missions. As far as I could tell, the only basis for their not being "really Methodist" related to what kind of Sunday school literature they bought, who they used as evangelists and what hymnbooks they sang from.

I was not in the ministry long before I realized there was a difference in the point of view expressed in the seminary classroom and by the Board of Ministerial Qualifications and that of the people in the churches I served. Music reveals cultural preferences, but even more important, it expresses our theological convictions and our religious heritage. As long as Methodists hold differing theological convictions and disagree about what their heritage is, they will have different opinions about music.

The United Methodist Church has a strong evangelical and revivalistic heritage. A significant part of the church is embarrassed by that heritage and would like for it to go away, or at least to be superseded. They would like to remold and resymbolize what has been passed down in order to make it "more relevant for the times."

Canadian hymnologist Charles Etherington expresses that point of view:

> To this day it is difficult to convince many Canadians (and perhaps Americans too) that gospel songs are not "good old Methodist hymns." Methodists may have had a hand in introducing such tunes, but they are not the hymns of Wesley. Continuing Methodists, and those who have merged into the United Church of Canada, are trying to live down this not wholly deserved reputation by decreasing the percentage of weak hymns with every revision of their hymnody.[1]

Thus the gap. On the one hand is the perspective taught me in seminary. The seminary made no attempt at evenhandedness. It was committed to "relevancy," academic solutions and whatever form of liberalism or neo-orthodoxy seemed popular at the moment. It looked with disfavor on simplistic answers, on too much emotion and on anything that culturally, educationally, socially or religiously might offend modern man. At times, it expressed embarrassment over Methodism's revivalistic heritage and its modern-day descendants, who were often characterized as fundamentalists or literalists.

On the other hand is common, ordinary Methodism (including the Evangelical United Brethren churches). Everyday Methodism, even though it has lost much of its forebears' enthusiasm, has continued to resist many of the efforts of the seminary-educated clergy and the church bureaucracies to retrain and redirect the church. Even when Methodism was no longer revivalistic, it carried over the cultural and theological preferences of its evangelical past. Those preferences, partly cultural and partly theological, express themselves in music and hymns.

Not long ago, I reexamined the hymnal that was used in the first church I served. The Union Chapel hymnal, the "unofficial" book that cast suspicion on its congregation's loyalty, had nearly twice as many actual Methodist authors as the official hymnal.

The (1935) official hymnal's "Holy, Holy, Holy" and "For the Beauty of the Earth" are Anglican hymns imported from England. "This Is My Father's World" came from a Presbyterian from the East. In contrast, unofficial hymns Union Chapel people loved to sing, such as "There Is Power in the Blood," "When the Roll Is Called Up Yonder I'll Be There" and "Jesus Paid It All," were written by Methodists and had grown out of Methodist experiences in camp meetings, Sunday schools and revivals.

In order to bring balance to discussions about Methodist music, it is helpful to trace Methodism's gospel heritage.

There should be no debate that any appreciation of Methodist music begins with a study of John and Charles Wesley and the role music played in the Methodist revival in England in the 1700s. The Wesleys' special gift was their ability to feel comfortable in cultured and academic circles while appealing to the masses. They combined within their own religious belief and practice both establishment Anglicanism and Methodist enthusiasm. And the music they introduced, Methodist music, linked together popular tunes, sophisticated poetry and orthodox and evangelical theology. Its genius was being evangelical in theology while at the same time reflecting the catholic nature of the church. It was relevant for its day, appealing to both rich and poor, educated and uneducated.

This is not to say that Methodist music was without critics. Establishment Anglicans were appalled by what the Methodists had introduced into English church life. Methodists were accused of unbridled enthusiasm and of disrupting the otherwise reserved and conservative worship life of the English.

Methodist tunes such as Diadem ("All Hail the Power of Jesus' Name" UMH #155) and Sagina (used in the 1989 UM hymnal with "And Can It Be That I Should Gain" #363) were considered outlandish and fanciful, bordering on hysterical. The British liked their tunes sedate.

When Methodist music reached the American shore it went in two directions. Many orthodox Methodists, located primarily along the Atlantic seaboard, faithfully followed Wesley's musical lead. If Wesley used British tunes, they used British tunes. If Wesley used hymns translated from the German Pietist tradition, they used such hymns. Any deviation from Wesley's music, particularly the recognition of ragged and uncouth frontier music, was discouraged.

However, alongside this music, and often competing against it, was the music of the frontier revival. This, too, was Methodist music, at least it originated with Methodists, was sung by Methodists and became a treasured part of the Methodist ethos (a way of thinking or acting).

To understand this music and its role in the development of Methodism, it is important to remember who the earliest American Methodists were. Methodists originally came from among America's common people. A good percentage were black, many were poor. Until 1784 they were little more than a sect, existing without benefit of clergy. Their leaders, such as they were, were hardly from America's aristocracy. No graduates of Yale or Harvard or Princeton were among the first preachers. Asbury had only a few years of formal training and many of his preachers had less.

Early American Methodists did appreciate John Wesley and his doctrines and discipline. They committed themselves to the Twenty-Five Articles of Religion and the connectional system of church government. At the same time, they felt no special ties to Wesley's politics (he was a Tory who wanted early Methodists to honor the King), or to his regard for Anglicanism. Wesley's white neck bands, his black gown and even the Sunday service authorized by Wesley for use by the Americans were widely disregarded, especially by frontier preachers.

Nevertheless, what Methodists lacked in wealth, education and refinement they made up for with zeal. They were "Spirit" Christians instead of "Word" Christians. The distinction is important. Early American Methodists did not emphasize the upholding of tradition, the fine points of Greek exegesis and the rational defense of the faith as much as the indwelling and guidance of the Holy Spirit. Early Methodism had a certain single-mindedness, centering on the preaching of redemption, the experience of the new birth and the expectation of heaven.

When that single-mindedness translated into a new Methodist ethos, it brought both creativity and excess. It meant a suspicion of the organized religion that was and the establishment of an organized religion that was to be.

The following is an excerpt from a much longer camp meeting spiritual that features a conversation between a Methodist and a Formalist about a Methodist meeting:

> **M:** Good morning, brother Pilgrim! What, trav'ling to Zion? What doubts and dangers have you met today? . . .
> **F:** I came out this morning, and now I'm returning,
> Perhaps little better than when I first came. . . .
> The preachers were stamping, the people were jumping,
> And screaming so loud that I nothing could hear,
> Either praying or preaching—such horrible shrieking!
> I was truly offended at all that was there.
> **M:** Perhaps, my dear brother, while they prayed together
> You sat and considered, but prayed not at all. . . .
> **F:** No place for reflection—I'm filled with distraction,
> I wonder that people could bear for to stay,
> These men they were bawling, the women were squalling,
> I know not for my part how any could pray. . . .
> **M:** Don't be so soon shaken—if I'm not mistaken
> Such things were perform'd by believers of old. . . .
> **F:** Then Scripture's contrasted, for Paul has protested
> That order should reign in the house of the Lord.
> **M:** . . . By your own confession you've made some impression,
> The sweet melting showers have soften'd your heart. . . .
> **F:** . . . My heart is now glowing! I feel his love flowing!
> Peace, pardon, and comfort I now do receive.[2]

What began happening almost immediately in the Methodist

revival was a burst of creative energy better suited to forming a new tradition and culture than passing on a heritage. The camp meeting gave evangelical church life the altar call, the mourner's bench, the song leader, the song evangelist, the all-night prayer meeting, the invitation hymn and the use of solos and special music as a part of religious gatherings. It also gave music such prominence in the religious meeting (it would be incorrect to call these "worship services") that it replaced the sermon as the focal point.

In the process, the Methodist revival illustrated one of Ernst Troeltsch's oft-quoted observations:

> The really creative, church-forming, religious movements are the work of the lower strata. . . . Need upon the one hand and the absence of an all-relativizing culture of reflection on the other hand are at home only in these strata. All great community-building revelations have come forth again and again out of such circles and the significance and power for further development in such religious movements have always been dependent upon the force of the original impetus.[3]

Musically, this meant the introduction of indigenous music. Watts and Wesley, and other evangelicals who carried the English revival, were sometimes replaced, at other times adapted and supplemented.

One early observer explained how this happened:

> At the commencement of the revival those familiar hymns [Wesley's], known in all our orthodox congregations, were used; but it was soon felt that they gave but imperfect expression to the ardent feelings of the worshipers. The deficiency was principally supplied by the preachers. Hymns, or "spiritual songs," as they were more frequently called, to the cultured ear rude and bold in expression, rugged in meter, and imperfect in rhyme, often improvised in the preaching stand, were at once accepted as more suited to their wants. These were quickly committed to memory, and to a c considerable extent usurped the place of the older and more worthy hymns.[4]

Thus was born the camp meeting spiritual, the forerunner of revival music, Sunday school music, Negro spirituals and gospel, whether black, contemporary or southern gospel. The camp meeting spiritual not only was influenced by the revival, but it also helped to bring about the revival. It, as much as the preaching, fueled revival fires. It also served to advance the Methodist cause.

> *The world, the devil and Tom Paine*
> *have try'd their force, but all in vain,*
> *they can't prevail, the reason is,*
> *the Lord defends the Methodist.*

> *They are despised by Satan's train,*
> *because they shout and preach so plain,*
> *I'm bound to march in endless bliss,*
> *and die a shouting Methodist.*
> (Early Methodist spiritual)

The authorship for almost all of the early Methodist spiritual songs is unknown. However, we do know about several authors. Caleb Jarvis Taylor and John Granade were Methodist preachers who compiled an early Methodist song book entitled *The Pilgrim's Songster.* First published in 1810, it sold at least ten thousand copies (amazing for that period). It included many of their own songs, as well as other indigenous American texts. Compared with the "fluff" of much contemporary gospel, these texts include some powerful images.

> *The battle, brethren, is begun!*
> *Behold the army now in motion!*
> *Some by faith behold the crown,*
> *And almost grasp their future portion.*
> *Hark! the victor's singing loud,*
> *Emmanuel's chariot wheels are rumbling:*
> *Mourners weeping through the crowd,*
> *And Satan's kingdom down is crumbling.*

One early observer, describing the hymns of Granade and Taylor, commented,

> It was not only at the meetings they were sung, but making so deep an impression upon the minds of the people of the period, they were soon learned by the thousands; who made the shops, the fields, the woods, the hills and the vales to echo with the melody of their voices. . . . When one was started at their meetings, hundreds would

unite, and being divided into many companies when singing would be going on, the sound of their voices 'was
heard afar off.' It was truly solemn and awful, yet
melodious! Under the singing the greatest power appeared generally to be displayed. Its charms disarmed and
then melted into tenderness the hard hearts of sinners.
Even the persecuting and heaven-daring sinner, would
sometimes have his attention caught by it, and be suddenly melted into tears; and at other times, seized with a
sudden trembling, they would fall to the ground.[5]

More sophisticated clergy greeted the popularity of this music
with a great deal of alarm. In the early 1800s it was possible to talk
about "Methodists" and "Formalists," but as Methodism prospered
and accumulated colleges and book concerns and ever stricter
ministerial qualifications, it began to react with some embarrassment to the rough and uncouth expressions of the revivalists.
Methodism was itself becoming "formal."

Bishops, as much as anyone, sensed these early tensions in the
church. In 1808 Bishop Francis Asbury, though he encouraged the
camp meeting and was himself a camp meeting preacher, wrote the
following warning:

We must therefore earnestly entreat you, if you have
any respect for the authority of the Conference, or of us,
or any regard for the prosperity of the Connection, to
purchase no Hymn-books, but what are signed with the
names of your Bishops.[6]

Thus Asbury, perhaps unwittingly, became one of the first
participants in the debate over what is appropriate music for
Methodists. On the one hand he wished to encourage the revival,
but on the other he saw the bishops as responsible for protecting
Methodist tradition and orthodoxy against excesses. Until recent
years, for most of Methodism's history, the signature of the bishops
was the authorization of an official Methodist hymnal.

To Do

Apart from Wesley texts, the following (condensed from
several sources) were among the most popular hymns sung by
early American Methodists, both in camp meeting and everyday

Methodist settings. Some are still used today, though probably with different tunes than were popular in early American Methodism.

1. Can you find the hymns? (Several are in older hymnals.)
2. What are the themes of the texts? How much emphasis is on heaven? On salvation? On present trials and tribulations?
3. How do the themes differ from the themes of our most-sung hymns today?

"Alas! and Did My Savior Bleed?" by Isaac Watts (UMH #359). From the beginning, this hymn has appeared in all Methodist hymnals, almost all of the frontier camp meeting songsters and most of the evangelical hymnals of today. It has been put to many tunes and has had various choruses attached to it. While many modern hymns have themes of creation and worship, this hymn (and others like it) speaks of a God of redemption and what our response to the world should be because of the cross.

Watts' original line "For such a worm as I" appeared in our hymnals until it was changed in the 1935 Methodist hymnal. The line now reads, "For sinners such as I."

"Jesus, My All, to Heaven Is Gone" by John Cennick. Cennick was a Calvinist British Methodist who wrote a number of hymns, including one we sometimes call "The Wesley Grace" ("Be present at our table, Lord"). Much of the attraction of "Jesus, My All, to Heaven Is Gone" was the tune "Duane Street," one of the most widely-sung tunes among country folk in the early 1800s. The hymn was sung less and less in the twentieth century and was dropped from the 1966 hymnal.

"Children of the Heavenly King" by John Cennick. This hymn, also by Cennick, was extremely popular in early Methodism and appeared in every hymnal until the present one.

"Come, Thou Fount of Every Blessing" by Robert Robinson (UMH #400). Many of the hymns popular among early Methodists were written by British authors but sung to American tunes. The tune "Nettleton" is one of the earliest American tunes to appear in our present hymnal. The text was sung to a number of other tunes in camp meeting settings. This hymn appears in almost all present-day evangelical hymnals.

"On Jordan's Stormy Banks I Stand" by Samuel Stennett (UMH #724). Another hymn that has been in all of our hymnals, the tune "Promised Land" is an early camp meeting tune. The theme of the hymn, heaven as the home beyond the Jordan, is one of the most common themes in early camp meeting music (especially in the black tradition).

"When I Can Read My Title Clear" by Isaac Watts. This is still a popular hymn in many evangelical churches. It was removed from Methodist hymnals in 1935 at a time when church liberals believed our hymns overemphasized heaven and life after death instead of the needs of the present world.

The original title for this hymn was "When I Can Read My Sentence Clear" (thus the theme of judgment and heaven). This has often been called the most popular and widely-sung hymn among blacks (both Methodist and non-Methodist) in the early years of our country. It was also Abraham Lincoln's favorite hymn.

"There Is a Fountain Filled with Blood" by William Cowper (UMH #622). Down through the years, this hymn has been criticized for its theology and its imagery (by those who oppose "blood" theology and imagery). On several occasions it was almost deleted from "official" hymnals, but it has remained simply because of its great popularity. It has been, from the beginning, a hymn popular with blacks.

The tune that we most generally associate with this hymn, "Cleansing Fountain," grew out of Methodism's camp meeting days. The hymn has, in fact, been so often associated with camp meetings that it is hymn #1 in several camp meeting songbooks and for years was the theme song and opening hymn for the national camp meeting movement.

Five

From Spiritual to Gospel

I was browsing in a used book store when I found it: *The Revivalist: A Collection of Choice Revival Hymns and Tunes, 1868.* I had read about this hymnal. It was one of the best sources for camp meeting tunes and early Methodist revival music. The "Cokesbury Hymnal" of its day, it contained many songs not found in the official hymnal which nevertheless were favorites among Methodist people. It was still a relatively rare book, despite the fact that *The Revivalist* sold 150,000 copies during its first four years of publication and went through eleven editions in that period of time. I had only seen the hymnal in a couple of seminary libraries. Purchasing it gave me the rush of a hobbyist's high.

Musically, *The Revivalist* was the link between American religious folk music on the frontier (the camp meeting spiritual) and the "gospel song" that soon became the mainstay of American evangelicalism. Joseph Hillman, who compiled *The Revivalist*, was a child of the popular Methodist culture that included camp meetings, revivals and "praying bands." His stated purpose was to gather old-time Methodist tunes and spiritual songs, many of which had never been written down. The book contains an endorsement written by Philip Phillips, music editor of the Methodist Book Concern and a song writer himself. The list of credits is a who's who of Methodist evangelists, song leaders and camp meeting enthusiasts. Even though they are not listed in Methodist encyclopedias as "distinguished leaders" in the church, they nevertheless made major contributions to the growth and power of early American Methodism.

The official hymnal of the Methodist Episcopal Church during the Civil War years dated from 1848. It was in many respects an excellent hymnal, orthodox in theology and consisting mostly of the hymns of Wesley. But it was not an American book. It was a British import, comfortable for that part of Methodism which was going respectable—Methodism of the cities, conservatories, organs, rented pews and robed clergy. Its tunes, which once were sung by Wesley followers on the greens and the fields of England, had become respected sanctuary music.

The Revivalist was the official hymnal's poor country cousin, reflecting a Methodism of camp meetings, log cabins, Sunday schools, mourners' benches and homemade pulpits. Like most Methodist-inspired "spiritual" songbooks of that era, it was intended to be a supplement to, not a substitute for, the official hymnal. The official book, signed by bishops, was for formal worship. Other books were designed for revivals and social occasions, which in that day included everything from class meetings and prayer bands to singing around the piano (when there was a piano) in the front parlor.

Many of the hymns of *The Revivalist*, though they did not appear in approved denominational hymnals at that time, are familiar to us today. Several, in fact, appear in our 1989 hymnal: "Amazing Grace," "Jesus Loves Me, This I Know," "Just As I Am, Without One Plea," "Sweet Hour of Prayer," "Shall We Gather at the River," "Must Jesus Bear the Cross Alone," "My Jesus, I Love Thee," "Savior, Like a Shepherd Lead Us," "Jesus, I My Cross Have Taken," "How Firm a Foundation," "Come, Every Soul by Sin Oppressed," "I Love to Tell the Story," "Revive Us Again," "Take the Name of Jesus With You" and "Jesus, Keep Me Near the Cross." Some are American texts. Others are British texts set to frontier tunes. *The Revivalist* made good use of the tunes of Lowell Mason and William Bradbury, both highly trained musicians who had a gift for writing and arranging music that was loved by American Christians.

This is not to suggest that *The Revivalist* was noted for respectability. Its Methodist music was exuberant, creative, crude, outlandish and quite different from anything that previously had been associated with religious music. Much of it was folk music of unknown origins, passed on by word of mouth. Many of its hymns have no credits. Others say "old tune" or "western melody."

The Revivalist contains the original form of "Come to Jesus," perhaps the most popular frontier invitation chorus before it was parodied as "O My Darling Clementine" and "Found a Peanut." The book lists several texts for "Say, Brothers," the original tune now better known as "The Battle Hymn of the Republic." Stephen Foster is shamelessly borrowed for religious purposes.

The texts in *The Revivalist* include sentimental stories about camping on the old campground (with an old military tune), seeing friends in heaven and mother's Bible.

> *This book is all that's left me now—*
> *tears will unbidden start—*
> *with falt'ring lip and throbbing brow,*
> *I press it to my heart.*
> *For many generations past,*
> *here is our fam'ly tree;*
> *my mother's hands this Bible clasp'd;*
> *she, dying, gave it me.*
> *(The Revivalist #330)*

Ballads in plaintive minor keys are offered in meters identified as "peculiar."

> *Review the palsied sinner's case*
> *who sought for help in Jesus;*
> *his friends conveyed him to the place*
> *where he might meet with Jesus.*
> *(The Revivalist #4)*

Dialogue songs abound.

> *What vessel are you sailing on?*
> *Pray tell to me its name.*
> *Our vessel is the Ark of God,*
> *And Christ our Captain's name.*
> *And what's the Port you're sailing to?*
> *Pray tell us all straightway;*
> *The new Jerusalem's the Port,*
> *The realms of endless day.*

With, of course, a rousing chorus added:

Then hoist every sail to catch the gale,
each sailor plies his oar;
the night begins to wear away,
we soon shall reach the shore.
(The Revivalist #408)

Methodists in *The Revivalist* sang unabashedly about blood-stained banners, the coming Jubilee, gospel ships, gospel trumpets, gospel feasts, and coming chariots, golden harps, Beulah land and Salem's happy ground.

They also sang Wesley and Watts. *The Revivalist* carried ninety-four Wesley texts and thirty-five by Isaac Watts. But it was Wesley with a difference, in frontier garb, with fuguing tunes (a complicated early American style in which different parts played against one another), minor keys, ragged meters and added choruses that were rousing and (to cultured ears) appalling. For example, a chorus with the familiar frontier pilgrim theme is added to Wesley's "Come, Sinners to the Gospel Feast":

O come and go along with me,
along with me, along with me,
O come and go along with me
away unto the promis'd land.

Another version of the same text adds the Methodist free grace theme:

Thro' grace, free grace,
Thro' grace, free grace,
To all the Jews and Gentile race.

Similar liberties were taken with the hymns of Isaac Watts. To Watts' "Alas! and Did My Savior Bleed" an emotional chorus is added that would have raised eyebrows among Watts' contemporaries:

I yield, I yield, I yield, I can hold out no more;
I sink, by dying love compell'd, And own thee conqueror.
(The Revivalist #443)

If that were not enough, another version of the same hymn adds a decidedly Methodist (and anti-Calvinist) chorus:

Yes, Jesus died for all mankind,
bless God he died for me.
(The Revivalist #319)

However the texts and tunes of *The Revivalist* might sound to us today, they were quite rambunctious for the mid-nineteenth century. Except for frontier Methodists and Baptists, religion in America was still characterized by propriety and reserve. Even Wesley was suspect. As one observer noted in 1859,

Many of the hymns which the Church cherishes as a peculiar sacred treasure, have been condemned . . . as too sensuous for the worship of a holy, spiritual being. Such strains as "Jesus, Lover of my Soul," jar upon the sensibilities made delicate by . . . culture.[1]

The continual crying out of the name "Jesus" seemed most inappropriate to many, and to use intimate terms of love and friendship with regard to Jesus was considered near sacrilege. Yet for frontier Methodists, the name of Jesus and expressions of love for Jesus became a focus in worship and music.

My Jesus, I love thee! I know thou art mine,
For thee all the pleasures of sin I resign.
(The Revivalist #79)

The origins of that revival favorite are obscure. *The Revivalist* carries that text and also an earlier version:

Oh, Jesus, my Saviuor! I know thou are mine;
For thee all the pleasures of earth I resign:
Of objects most pleasing, I love thee the best;
Without thee I'm wretched, but with thee I'm blest.
(The Revivalist #342)

To this a chorus can be added:

I love thee, I love thee, I love thee, my Lord,
I love thee, my Saviour, I love thee, my God;
But how much I love thee I never can show.
I love thee, I love thee, and that thou dost know.

(A form of this chorus appears in evangelical hymnals of today.)

This seemed like unbridled sentimentality to many. Even the children's favorite, "Jesus Loves Me," (which appears in five languages in the new hymnal) was deemed inappropriate by some and for many years did not appear in an official hymnal.

> *Jesus loves me! this I know,*
> *for the Bible tells me so. (UMH #191)*

The following is another popular Methodist chorus (especially among blacks) that appears in the new hymnal. It has been used with many different texts, but appeared in *The Revivalist* with Wesley's "Jesus! the Name High over All" (#456).

> *O how I love Jesus,*
> *O how I love Jesus,*
> *O how I love Jesus,*
> *because he first loved me.*
> *(UMH #170)*

In addition to the criticism that Methodist revival hymns were on overly intimate terms with a holy God, many people felt that the hymns were too emotional. This was especially true of the "invitation" hymns. Behind Methodism's cry of "free grace" was the belief that God's prevenient grace meant any person—rich or poor, black or white, old or young—could be saved. The gospel message, therefore, whether preached or sung, was often directed to the lost. Thus in Wesley's hymns, we sing,

> *Come, sinners, to the gospel feast. (UMH #339)*

and,

> *Sinners, turn: why will you die? (UMH #346)*

Calvinists (including Presbyterians and early Baptists), because of their views on predestination, believed that invitation hymns assumed a too-easy access to God's grace. Methodist invitational hymns, however, were at the heart of the revival. What Calvinists considered "too-easy access" was "free grace" to Methodists.

> *Come, every soul by sin oppressed,*
> *there's mercy in the Lord;*
> *and he will surely give you rest,*

by trusting in his Word.
(UMH #337)

The original chorus in *The Revivalist,* by the Methodist camp meeting evangelist, J.H. Stockton, went,

Come to Jesus, Come to Jesus,
Come to Jesus now!
He will save you, He will save you,
He will save you now.
(The Revivalist #500)

Those words became so over-used in Methodist and revival circles that a few years later Ira Sankey wrote a new chorus, the one in our hymnal today:

Only trust him, only trust him,
only trust him now.
He will save you, he will save you,
he will save you now. (UMH #337)

Whether highly regarded or not, the songs of *The Revivalist* were the songs that were sung by ordinary Methodists, Evangelicals and United Brethren. The choruses could be learned without benefit of a hymnal. The tunes were singable. The texts, though not as profound as those offered by more sophisticated poets, were understandable. Their messages reflected the straightforward Methodist theology of the day.

In camp meetings and revivals, prayer bands and class meetings, missionary meetings and informal gatherings in homes, this was the music that brought sinners to repentance and strengthened believers in times of trial. It represented catechism and creed and gave Methodism an identity.

But this music was also—and this cannot be overstressed—an embarrassment for many. Not all Methodists were poor, rural, given to holiness prayer meetings or caught up in revivals. Second-generation Methodists on the frontier became distinguished citizens who demanded educated clergy, orderly worship and tasteful music. Log cabin churches and small white frame buildings were often replaced by imposing brick structures with stained glass windows and steeples. Organs and robed choirs were introduced in churches. Revival excesses and glory shouts were unbecoming in such settings. Methodists were moving up the social scale.

This resulted in a cultural (and later, a theological) gap. Originally the gap was between the style and temperament of the urban, sophisticated East and the rough revivalism of the frontier West. The cultured East was (at that time) conservative and resistent to change. The revivalism of the West was reformist, experimental and daring.

Musically, the urban churches were highly committed to the hymns of Wesley and the culture of England. In contrast, the frontier churches sang the camp meeting spirituals and the revival songs that grew out of the American experience. The cultural background of the Evangelical and United Brethren churches was German instead of English, but the gap was developing just the same.

Official hymnals belonged to the cultured East. The Methodist Episcopal hymnal of 1848 did not contain even one of the popular camp meeting spirituals. Only two of its thousand-plus hymns were written by Americans (Robert West, "Come, Let Us Tune Our Loftiest Song," and Timothy Dwight, "I Love Thy Kingdom, Lord"). As far as the official hymnal was concerned, it was as though the Methodist revival sweeping the nation did not exist.

Meanwhile scores of Methodist-inspired songbooks were issued. Ellen Jane Lorenz has identified at least forty-two of these, issued between 1811 and 1875, of which *The Revivalist* was the best known.[2]

The struggle over music reflected a larger struggle for the soul of the church. German higher criticism of the Bible began making inroads into Methodist circles by the 1870s. The publishing of Horace Bushnell's *Christian Nurture* in 1858 introduced the belief that children needed education, not conversion, to become Christians.

Revivalism itself was undergoing change. Originally optimistic, reformist and post-millennial (the view that the world would be won to Christ through an outpouring of God's Spirit and that Christ's Second Coming would follow a period of universal peace), evangelical Christianity became increasingly pessimistic (and eventually pre-millennial) following the Civil War. Furthermore, evangelical Methodists found themselves increasingly alienated within the structures of their own denomination.

The Methodist Episcopal General Conference that authorized the official hymnal of 1878 was conducted without benefit of laity, women or blacks. Almost none of the delegates were circuit preachers or evangelists. Like many General Conferences, the clergymen elected to offices were the kind described in Methodist encyclopedias as "distinguished," "eminent" and "prominent." *The Methodist Quarterly Review* describes the committee selected to compile the new hymnal as men of

> local distinction as poets, and even national reputation as composers . . . college presidents, professors, presiding elders, a pastor, and one lawyer, [who] were representatives of distinct classes of culture, position, and experience.[3]

It was a foregone conclusion that such a committee would not be sympathetic to spiritual songs and revival choruses—the music of common Methodists. Of 307 authors in the 1878 hymnal, there were 66 Episcopalians, 22 Congregationalists, 20 Presbyterians, 14 Unitarians, 13 Lutherans and 13 Roman Catholics. Only ten were members of the Methodist Episcopal Church, and none of the ten was from the denomination's revival or holiness wing. Only seven percent of the hymns were of American origin. Out of 1,117 hymns, only three were identified with anyone west of Rochester, New York, or south of Washington, D.C. Only three hymns in the entire hymnal carried a refrain or chorus (the sign of a gospel song).

The noted hymnologist Louis Benson made this comment about the hymnal:

> . . . it had hardly appeared before complaints began that it served better as a collection of devotional poetry than as a congregational hymn book. The church hymn book became less than ever a bond of unity and means of uniformity in worship, and served many dissatisfied pastors and ambitious compilers as a point of departure.[4]

The M.E. South hymnal of 1889 was only slightly more diverse. Of 258 authors, 55 were Church of England, 25 were Presbyterian, 25 were Baptist and 15 were American Methodist.

Twenty percent of its authors were women (as opposed to seven percent of the M.E. hymnal). The southern church did authorize a supplement of 76 hymns for use in "prayer meetings and Sunday schools" that included a number of the popular "gospel songs."

Although the 1889 hymnal sold 576,000 copies in its first edition, within ten years it had fallen into such disuse that the church was clamoring for still another hymnal.

These hymnals were harbingers of the future direction of Methodism. In a denomination where being "official" meant being blessed, and being "unofficial" meant blessing was withheld, it was evident that the blessing and the power belonged to those "prominent," "eminent" and "distinguished" men from "the distinct classes of culture and position." Poor people, blacks, revivalists and the holiness evangelists would have to fend for themselves.

And so they did. A portion of Methodism found itself increasingly drawn to organizations outside the official structures of the church: the YMCA (at that time an evangelical organization), holiness associations, camp meeting associations (at places such as Ocean Grove, N.J., Round Lake, N.Y. and Vineland, N.J.), Sunday school associations, inner city missions and other independent missions organizations.

For a period of time, these independent movements were rallying points for much of the evangelical wing of the church. From 1867 to 1883, a total of fifty-two National Camp Meetings were held, mostly on Methodist campgrounds. The meeting at Round Lake, N.Y., in 1874 attracted twenty thousand worshipers and seven bishops. By 1888, four publishing houses were devoted exclusively to the dissemination of holiness literature.

At first, the institutional church reacted to the holiness movement and other "unofficial" organizations with support, then caution, then charges of disloyalty. As one critic wrote in 1885,

> ... they sing different songs; they patronize and circulate a different literature; they have adopted radically different words of worship. ... [5]

In 1894 the General Conference of the M.E. Church South took a strong anti-holiness stand, starting what some later called the "war of extermination." In both the North and South, a movement began to bring music, literature, mission work, revival meetings and camp meetings under denominational control.

As a result, Methodism lost its poor. The underclass, which had been disdained by other denominations but welcomed by the followers of Wesley, was feeling increasingly isolated from the church that had once nourished them in faith.

This caused a splintering and an exodus from Methodism, creating what is known as the Holiness, Pentecostal and Charismatic movements today. It is impossible to trace the number of groups, sects and denominations that arose between 1880 and 1923 that had roots in Methodism or Methodist teaching. One observer notes that no less than two hundred such groups using some form of the name "Church of God" alone sprang up during that period.[6]

The Salvation Army, organized in America in 1880, was committed to the poor as well as Wesleyan doctrines. The Church of the Nazarene can be traced to P. F. Bresee, a Methodist preacher who worked among the poor in Los Angeles in 1894. The Assembly of God organized in 1914. One of the largest black pentecostal groups, the Church of God in Christ, dates to 1897 (this group was an integrated denomination until the 1920s). It's interesting to note that the religious ferment of the 1890s had much in common with the political and sociological movement known as "populism." Populism was a protest against "Eastern establishment" ideology that led to the presidential candidacy of William Jennings Bryan.

Despite the splintering away of groups during this period, Methodism still dominated the American religious scene. At the turn of the twentieth century, there were still more Methodists than any other denominational family group. In spite of its growing sophistication, Methodism's message still appealed to all kinds of people—rich and poor, old and young, black and white, liberal and evangelical.

Musically, Methodists continued to contribute to American evangelical Christianity. They carried on the tradition of the Wesley hymns, and, with Baptists, played a major part in the evolution of the "gospel hymn" (see next chapter) and black gospel. Many of the spiritual songs and choruses in the camp meeting tradition were passed on to the Pentecostal and Charismatic groups, only to return to the mainstream in the 1970s and 1980s in the form of "Scripture songs," "praise songs" or "worship songs."

To Do

The chorus is associated with frontier camp meetings and revivals. It was introduced at a time when not everyone had hymnbooks, and when, because of the nature of the times, people preferred catchy tunes and verses easily memorized. The chorus was an important part of the Methodist ethos during this period.

The chorus originally was not intended for formal worship, being better suited for camp settings, Sunday schools and informal gatherings.

In recent years, the chorus moved into the sanctuary. In many ways, choruses function like the sung congregational responses in formal services. They are part of the call to worship, the invitation to prayer or the benediction. But choruses have assumed an additional function in some churches: They have become a major expression of praise and adoration in the worship service.

Choruses have sometimes been associated with the charismatic renewal movement, but it is a mistake to associate choruses only with charismatic worship. Variously known as Scripture songs or worship choruses, this music is often used by churches wanting a different style of music to reach youth and young adults.

Some have called this "heads up" music, as opposed to "heads down" music. Heads up music may rely on an overhead projector to free the worshiper from reliance on hymnals and bulletins.

Several choruses included in the 1989 hymnal are:

"Thank You, Lord" (UMH #84)
"Blessed Be the Name"(UMH #63)
"To God Be the Glory" (Crouch) (UMH #99)
"El Shaddai" (UMH #123)
"Alleluia" (UMH #186)
"He Is Lord, He Is Lord" (UMH #177)
"His Name Is Wonderful" (UMH #174)
"Jesus, Jesus, Jesus" (UMH #171)
"Emmanuel, Emmanuel" (UMH #204)
"Turn Your Eyes upon Jesus" (UMH #349)
"Seek Ye First" (UMH #405)
"Majesty, Worship His Majesty" (UMH #176)

1. How do you feel about the use of these songs in worship?
2. How will these be used in your church?
3. Are choruses here to stay, or are they a passing fad?

Six

Gospel Music
and the
Methodists

One day in the 1890s, Bessie, a fourteen-year-old girl in Williamsport, Pennsylvania, was invited to a Methodist Sunday school and young people's group at the Methodist church. She could not come, she replied, because she did not have suitable clothes. Her father was an alcoholic and there was no money in the home. The man who had invited her, James Black, made sure some clothes were found, and soon Bessie was a regular attender at the Methodist church.

Bessie was absent one day, though, at a special meeting of the Epworth League. The roll was called, but she did not answer.

Bessie had pneumonia and died several days later. The thought of Bessie and the missed roll call stuck in the mind of James Black, the teacher. From that experience, he wrote a song about a different kind of roll call:

> When the trumpet of the Lord shall sound
> and time shall be no more,
> and the morning breaks eternal, bright and fair;
> when the saved of earth shall gather over on the other-
> shore,
> when the roll is called up yonder, I'll be there.

I remember another Bessie—our cook in the commons at seminary. Bessie brought the exuberance of her black church into her daily work. She exhorted her "preacher boys" and sang her faith, sometimes accompanied by banging on pans, while working in the kitchen. One of her favorites was "When the Roll Is Called Up Yonder." Seminarians otherwise restrained and inhibited by formal religion were freed in Bessie's presence to sing along and express an often repressed portion of Methodist tradition.

I can recall another time when James Black's song was an important part of my Methodist experience. I accompanied a team of thirty United Methodist youth, some of whom were already caught up in the tumultuous spirit of the 1960s, to Haiti for a work camp and tour. The young Christians were moved by the Haitian church's program, people and culture. But the worship in the Haitian churches, particularly the singing, made the greatest impact on the youth. One favorite that was sung over and over, usually accompanied by hand-clapping, was "When the Roll Is Called Up Yonder." The music seemed, in the words of one teenager, "really relevant." One girl remarked, "Why don't we ever have any neat music like that in our churches?" The song became the theme of several presentations the group did when they returned home.

The text of "When the Roll Is Called Up Yonder" is hardly a literary classic, and the music is not memorable. The song is a typical gospel hymn. But, for good or ill, it represents an important chapter in the United Methodist story.

If camp meeting spirituals, Sunday school songs and choruses characterized grass-roots Methodism in the years 1800-1870, Methodism from 1870-1920 was known for the gospel hymn. James Black was by no means the best-known or the greatest of the gospel hymn writers or compilers, but he epitomizes the tradition.

Black was a layperson, active in Sunday school work and in the social outreach of the church. He saw gospel hymns as a means of presenting the truths of the faith in a simple, straightforward, understandable manner. He edited more than a dozen gospel songbooks, one of which, *Songs of the Soul,* published in 1894, sold 400,000 copies. He was respected enough to be chosen to serve on the hymnal revision committee of 1905, though none of his own hymns were selected for that book.

Black was just one of a number of Methodists committed to

compiling and publishing gospel music. Philip Phillips, musical editor of the Methodist Book Concern for many years, edited *Musical Leaves*, which sold one million copies, and *Singing Pilgrim*, which sold 800,000.

Henry Shephard Date (1858-1915) founded Hope Publishing Company and published "Pentecostal Hymns," a series of songbooks popular in Methodist churches (and those of other denominations) in the 1890s and well into the twentieth century. Like most Methodist hymnwriters and compilers of that period, Date was active on the camp meeting and revival circuit as a preacher and singer. He is also known as the founder and first president of the Young People's Alliance, the forerunner of the Epworth League.

William James Kirkpatrick (1838-1921) was a composer as well as a compiler. In addition to serving as a choir director in Methodist churches in the Philadelphia area, Kirkpatrick was president of the Praise Publishing Company. He compiled more than one hundred songbooks with total sales running into the millions. Some of the still-popular hymns he composed include "Lead Me to Calvary," "Jesus Saves," "He Hideth My Soul," "O To Be Like Thee," "'Tis So Sweet to Trust in Jesus" and "Redeemed."

During the golden era of gospel music—1870 to 1920—Methodism (including United Brethren and Evangelical churches) was fast becoming the American culture religion. On one level, in its General Conferences, the books of its publishing company and its colleges, the church was a growing respectable and "establishment." Methodist worship was becoming less exuberant and more formal. Its members were climbing the sociological scale and were increasingly identified as community leaders. The church was looking with disapproval on its holiness and revivalist wing, and becoming more and more fascinated by secular learning. The drift (perhaps "slide" is a better word) toward political liberalism and theological modernism was unmistakable.

On another level, however, Methodism still could attract the masses. Its Sunday schools, camp meetings and revivals continued to thrive. The Methodists, along with the Baptists, dominated America's small towns and rural areas. Not all of its pastors had been educated out of their zeal. On this level, gospel music was a glue that bound together evangelical style and substance. Gospel music gave an identity to common, ordinary Methodism, and was in turn influenced by Methodist and Baptist ways of preaching and teaching.

The phrase "gospel hymn" was introduced to the evangelical world by a Methodist Sunday school superintendent, Ira Sankey. On an October day in 1870, in Indianapolis, Indiana, Sankey led an otherwise dull YMCA gathering in the singing of "There Is a Fountain Filled with Blood." The featured speaker, Dwight L. Moody, was so moved by the singing he asked Sankey on the spot to join him in full-time evangelistic work.

Sankey did, launching the evangelistic ministry of the team of Moody and Sankey. This ministry eventually touched every major city in America and Great Britain and became the model for evangelistic teams even to the present day.

Like the Wesley revival in England and the camp meeting revival in America, the Moody-Sankey crusades used music both to attract crowds and proclaim the gospel. The singing, as well as the preaching, touched the heart. The songs that Sankey sang as solos or used with choirs or congregations were the songs people hummed while riding city trolleys or performing chores in country barns. Hymns in our present hymnal like "What a Friend We Have in Jesus," "Savior, Like a Shepherd Lead Us" and "Revive Us Again" are carry-overs from Moody-Sankey crusades.

More importantly, Sankey popularized a style of music that, for good or ill, has left its mark on the evangelical church to the present time. Not all in the church were (or are) pleased. Like Christian rock music today, gospel hymns were criticized for being too similar to the music of the secular world. As Dr. H.M. Poteat wrote in 1921,

> Perhaps the chief reason . . . for the popularity of the cheap 'hymn' is to be found in the fondness for secular music of the same type, which seems to be so characteristic of our time. Blues, jazz, waltzes, ragtime, slushy sentimentality have become the musical expression of so many people outside the church, that the same sort of thing, with a poor, thin veneer of religion, is demanded in the church.[1]

While critics railed at Sankey's music and Moody's preaching, common people heard them gladly. It is said that 2,500,000 attended the Moody crusades in England in four months in 1875. The largest crowd ever assembled in New York's history heard Sankey's songs at the New York Hippodrome during the 1876 Christian Convention.

Soon the Sankey songs were being sung across the nation, in parks, in churches, along country roads. They were published in *Gospel Hymns No. 1 to 6*, the sales of which reached fifty million copies.

Philip Phillips, Lewis Hartsough, William Hunter, William G. Fischer, Mary Kidder, William McDonald, Mrs. Joseph Knapp, Mary Lathbury, Elisha Hoffman (of the Evangelical Church), E.S. Lorenz (United Brethen), William Kirkpatrick and Frank Bottome are just a few of the Methodist preachers, evangelists, song leaders and Sunday school teachers whose works found ready acceptance though Sankey's efforts.

A few of these, along with their songs, deserve special mention. The name most frequently identified with gospel music and the Sankey style is Fanny Crosby. It has been said that Fanny Crosby (1820-1915), along with Ira Sankey and Dwight L. Moody, did more to set the direction of evangelicalism in the last quarter of the nineteenth century than any other person. Blinded at six weeks of age by improper medical treatment, Fanny Crosby wrote her first poem at age eight. A lifelong member of St. John's Methodist Church in New York, Fanny Crosby knew almost all of the gospel writers and singers of her day—Philip Phillips, William Bradbury, William Doane, William Kirkpatrick and others.

But Sankey, a fellow Methodist, became her greatest supporter. Fifty-nine hymns by Fanny Crosby appear in Sankey's *Gospel Hymns 1 to 6*. "Pass Me Not, O Gentle Savior," "I Am Thine, O Lord," "Blessed Assurance," "Rescue the Perishing," "To God Be the Glory," "Thou, My Everlasting Portion" and "Jesus, Keep Me Near the Cross" are the Fanny Crosby hymns appearing in the 1989 United Methodist hymnal.

Every one of Fanny Crosby's hymns has a story behind it. Many grew out of experiences related to inner city mission work in New York. Crosby frequently spoke at such missions. At one speaking engagement, after an appeal to remember a mother's home and teaching, a young man came forward to accept Christ.

His remark that night, "Now I can meet my mother in heaven, for I have found God," inspired the gospel song:

> *Rescue the perishing, care for the dying,*
> *snatch them in pity from sin and the grave;*
> *weep o'er the erring one, lift up the fallen,*
> *tell them of Jesus, the mighty to save. (UMH #591)*

Other gospel songs by Methodist writers in the Sankey era came out of missionary settings. Louisa Stead (1850-1917) wrote,

> *'Tis so sweet to trust in Jesus,*
> *and to take him at his word.*
> *(UMH #462)*

during a time of personal difficulty when she was a missionary in South Africa. At the time, she wrote in a letter: "Who is sufficient for these things? But with simple confidence and trust we may and do say, 'Our sufficiency is of God.'" "'Tis So Sweet to Trust in Jesus" became as popular in Africa as it was in America. Louisa Stead's last years were spent at Umtali, a well-known missionary station in Rhodesia (now Zimbabwe). At her death, a missionary commented, "We miss her very much, but her influence goes on as our five thousand native Christians continually sing this hymn in their native tongue."

Another Methodist who worked closely with Moody and Sankey was the composer William G. Fischer. He wrote the music to Katherine Hankey's "I Love To Tell the Story." His other well-known tunes include "Whiter Than Snow" and "I Am Trusting Lord in Thee."

One composer and author whose hymns were used by Sankey became a publisher in his own right. Elisha Hoffman (1839-1929) was part of the UM tradition through the Evangelical Church, serving with its publishing house in Cleveland for eleven years. Hoffman wrote two thousand hymns, including "Are You Washed in the Blood?" "Is Your All on the Altar?" "What a Wonderful Savior," "Leaning on the Everlasting Arms," "Glory to His Name" and "I Must Tell Jesus."

Although many musicians predicted that the gospel hymn would lose favor with the passing of Moody and Sankey, gospel music became more, not less, integral to Protestant evangelicalism as it entered the twentieth century.

Judson W. Van De Venter (1855-1939) wrote "All to Jesus I Surrender" (UMH #354) while struggling to decide whether to commit to being a full-time Methodist evangelist. Thomas O. Chisholm (1866-1960) wrote "Great Is Thy Faithfulness" (UMH #140) out of his personal realization of God's morning by morning steadfastness. Chisholm, a Methodist minister, was converted under the influence of Dr. Henry Clay Morrison, founder of Asbury Theological Seminary. He also was responsible for the hymn "Living for Jesus," as well as "He Was Wounded for Our Transgressions," "Christ Is Risen From the Dead" and "O to Be Like Thee!"

Perhaps the most popular twentieth-century gospel hymn was written by another Methodist pastor and evangelist, George Bennard (1873-1958). The hymn is "On a Hill Far Away" (UMH #504) ("The Old Rugged Cross"). Its message reflects the prominent place that preaching about the cross occupied in the Methodist revivals of the early twentieth century.

Homer Rodeheaver was another well-known Methodist who influenced the development of gospel music. Rodeheaver is best known not as a composer or author, but as a song evangelist, publisher and popularizer of music. Rodeheaver was associated with Billy Sunday and the Sunday-Rodeheaver evangelistic crusades of 1910-1920. Through those crusades, songs like "I Serve a Risen Savior" and "In the Garden" became gospel hymn favorites across the country.

The controversy between Methodists who preferred the gospel music of Fanny Crosby and Ira Sankey and those who favored a more formal style of hymnody that stressed "better" music and "finer" poetry was faced in the 1905 Methodist hymnal. The hymnal was a joint effort of the M.E. Church and the M.E. Church South and was compiled by a committee which, like the committees before it, consisted primarily of "prominent," "distinguished" and "eminent" men.

The editor of the hymnal, commenting on the "gospel song," the "spiritual song" and the "pennyroyal," wrote that while all Methodists believe in enthusiasm, Methodism "should never, we all agree, encourage a poor sinner or feeble saint to base enthusiasm on a bubble, a rattle, or a jingle."

However, about thirty bubbles, rattles and jingles were added to the book (out of 748 selections) as a compromise. This was the first significant inclusion of revival or gospel music in any official Methodist hymnal. The rest of the collection, besides Wesley (whose stock was falling with each new hymnal), relied heavily on Anglican divines and Unitarian poets. Eighty-two percent of the hymns were of British or European origin, as if that were the place to find true religion. In addition to the heavy infiltration of the Unitarians, there were more Congregational, Presbyterian and Episcopalian authors than those of the M.E. Church South, and almost as many as from the M.E. Church North.

While many of the gospel hymns and gospel publishing houses were associated with the midwest (particularly Chicago), fewer than ten of the 748 hymns in the 1905 hymnal were linked with anyone west of Rochester, New York, or south of Washington, D.C. It was an Eastern, elitist, establishment hymnal.

The hymnal also symbolized the struggle taking place for the soul of the church. On one side were those who wished to move the church away from and beyond its gospel, revival and evangelical past toward a more cultured, educated and liberal stance. So there would be no mistaking where the bishops stood, the statement signed by them in the hymnal's preface stated that the publishing of the hymnal meant any unauthorized books, "which often teach what organized Methodism does not hold, and which, by excluding the nobler music of the earlier and later days, prevent the growth of a true musical taste," should be supplanted. The arch supporters of this perspective even objected to the thirty gospel hymns, saying the hymnal was compromised by "a few cheap, ephemeral, jingly ditties."[2]

On the other side were those who claimed that the new hymnal served the interests of the few and not the many. A hymnal was hardly a standard work if it did not use the standard hymns people were acquainted with. Some pointed out that as unacceptable as the 1889 hymnal of the M.E. Church South was, it at least had a supplement of seventy-six hymns that were usable for Sunday schools and prayer meetings. In the northern church, an "authorized" (meaning it had official sanction) Sunday school book (*Epworth Hymnal* #1) had been approved by the 1884 General Conference. These, as well as other hymnals, would not be easily "supplanted." Within a few years after 1905, reports were circulated of churches with "Methodist hymnals lying unused in the pews."

Largely for this reason, a compromise was reached. The first Cokesbury Hymnal was published in 1923. Selling a million copies in the southern church alone, it was a hymnal for churches who preferred a different style of music in their Sunday schools or evening services. Cokesbury hymnals drew heavily on "Rodeheaver hymns" and were the first semi-official hymnals to include Negro spirituals.

In 1925, the Sunday School Board of the M.E. Church South surveyed 2,209 Methodist churches to discover what primary hymnal was being used in Sunday schools. The results were discouraging: 111 different titles were listed. Eleven of the titles had some official Methodist connection, implying approval, but one hundred were gospel books from independent publishers. Only eight percent of the churches (179 of 2,209) used the Methodist hymnal. Thirty-three percent (737 of 2,209) used the Cokesbury Hymnal.

To Do

Ironies abound in hymnody. One irony is that much "Methodist music," that is, music that grew out of the popular Methodist ethos, never found its way into official Methodist hymnals. Instead, it is found in independently published hymnals or in the hymnals of other evangelical denominations. For example, the new Broadman hymnal (Southern Baptist) carries many more hymns by American Methodists than does *The United Methodist Hymnal.*

What are examples of this music? Following is a partial list from the Broadman hymnal. These are in addition to the hymns written by Methodists already mentioned in this chapter (almost all of which are also in the Broadman hymnal).

1. How many of the hymns listed below do you know?

2. During what era were most of the hymns written?

3. What does the inclusion of so much Methodist music in a Baptist hymnal say about Methodists of a hundred years ago and today, and Baptists of a hundred years ago and today?

"A Wonderful Savior Is Jesus My Lord" by Fanny Crosby. Fanny Crosby, who has already been discussed, has thirteen hymns in the Broadman hymnal (seven of hers appear in the 1989 United Methodist hymnal.

"Are You Weary, Are You Heavyhearted?" ("Tell It To Jesus") music by E.S. Lorenz (1854-1942), editor of United Brethren hymnals and prolific gospel hymn writer. This hymn was originally written in German. Lorenz hymns and arrangements dominated United Brethren hymnals before the United Brethren and Evangelical merger. Nevertheless, the EUB hymnal of 1955 contained no Lorenz hymns.

"Down at the Cross Where My Savior Died" by Elisha Hoffman (1839-1929), of the Evangelical Church. Hoffman's hymns can be found in many hymnals besides the Southern Baptist hymnal. "Down at the Cross" was first published in the book *Joy to the World* (1878); one of the compilers of this songbook was C.C. McCabe (later a bishop). Four Hoffman hymns appear in the Broadman hymnal.

"Face to Face with Christ, My Savior" tune by Grant Tullar (1869-1950). The hymn was inspired by a Methodist revival in Rutherford, New Jersey, in 1898.

"I Am So Happy in Christ Today" a hymn inspired by a Methodist revival in Waycross, Georgia, in 1909. One of those who professed faith in Christ at this meeting was Arthur Moore, later a Methodist bishop.

"Jesus Paid It All" by Elvina Hall (1820-1889). Mrs. Hall wrote the song after an especially inspiring service at Monument Street Methodist Church in Baltimore.

"I Hear Thy Welcome Voice" by Lewis Hartsough, (1828-1919). Inspiration for the hymn came from a Methodist revival in Epworth, Iowa.

"If You Are Tired of the Load of Your Sin" by Mrs. C.H. Morris (1862-1929). This hymn grew out of an experience in 1898 at Mountain Lake Camp Meeting. The Broadman hymnal also carries Mrs. Morris' hymn, "Jesus Is Coming to Earth Again." Mrs. Morris originally came from the Methodist Protestant tradition. She authored several thousand hymns.

"I'm Pressing on the Upward Way" by Johnson Oatman Jr. (1856-1922). Oatman has four hymns in the Baptist hymnal. What is unusual about finding this hymn (also known as "Higher Ground") in a Baptist hymnal is that it is (or was) an explicitly

Methodist camp meeting hymn written to express the Methodist doctrine of holiness.

"I Am Coming to the Cross" by William McDonald (1820-1901). This hymn of invitation appeared in United Methodist hymnals until the 1989 hymnal. McDonald was for many years associated with the National Holiness Association, and the hymn is a holiness hymn. Its appearance in the Broadman hymnal demonstrates how such music has influence far beyond Methodist circles.

"In Times Like These " by Ruth Caye Jones (1902-1972). This is one example of a gospel hymn written by a Methodist in more recent times.

"I've Wandered Far Away from God" by William Kirkpatrick (1838-1921). Kirkpatrick is identified with eight hymns in the Broadman hymnal, mostly with tunes. "I've Wandered Far Away from God" ("Lord, I'm Coming Home") has been popularized in recent years by George Beverly Shea.

"Jesus, Friend of Thronging Pilgrims" a hymn originally written for a Methodist Council of Bishops Convocation on Urban Life.

"Living for Jesus" by T.O. Chisholm (1866-1960). Chisholm also wrote "Great Is Thy Faithfulness."

"Lord Jesus, I Long To Be Perfectly Whole " ("Whiter Than Snow") by James Nicholson (1828-1876). Nicholson was also associated with revivals and camp meetings. The tune is by another Methodist, William Fischer (1835-1912).

"Of the Themes that Men Have Known" by Albert Fisher (1838-1912). Fisher, Methodist pastor and evangelist from Texas, has two hymns in the Broadman hymnal.

"Sing the Wondrous Love of Jesus" (When We All Get to Heaven") one of many gospel songs affiliated with Ocean Grove Camp meeting in New Jersey. The composer was Emily D. Wilson (1865-1942).

"Send the Light" by Charles Gabriel (1856-1932). He wrote the hymn for the Easter service of Grace M.E. Church in San Francisco in 1890 when he was church chorister there. Gabriel has ten hymns (mostly tunes) in the Broadman hymnal. Gabriel was also associated with camp meetings. He was the music editor for the Epworth League hymnal, one of a number of semi-official

Methodist songbooks that drew from Methodism's revival and camp meeting heritage.

"There's Within My Heart a Melody" ("He Keeps Me Singing") by Luther Bridgers (1884-1948). Bridgers was a Methodist pastor from Georgia. He wrote the hymn after a tragic fire took the lives of his wife and children while he was away holding revival services.

"Jesus Saves" by Priscilla Owens (1829-1907). A number of her hymns appear in hymnbooks of the Sankey era.

"We Thank Thee that Thy Mandate" by Ernest K. Emurian, a Methodist pastor who has written several studies on hymns.

"Walking in Sunlight, All of My Journey" ("Heavenly Sunlight") by Henry Zelley (1859-1942). This hymn was popularized by Charles E. Fuller and the Old Fashioned Revival Hour radio broadcast.

"When the Roll Is Called Up Yonder I'll Be There " by James Black (discussed earlier in this chapter).

"There's Power in the Blood" by Lewis Jones (1865-1936). Both author and hymn were identified with the Mountain Lake Camp Meeting.

Seven

The Liberal Reaction

The 1935 Methodist hymnal was introduced to the church amid rave reviews. The hymnal represented, to borrow a phrase from the Hymn Society of America, "new words for a new day." This meant it was in tune with science and modern culture and was committed to modernism and the social gospel. Local Methodist churches might cling to traditional worship styles and theology, but, it was argued, the future was liberalism, and the new hymnal reflected that future.

An analysis of the 1935 hymnal confirms the suspicion that some radical theological redirection had taken place. To illustrate:

1. The number of Wesley hymns continued to be reduced, from 558 in the 1849 hymnal to 121 in the 1905 hymnal to 56 in the 1935 hymnal. Some people commented that the church needed to move beyond Wesley.

2. Sections on "The Need for Salvation," "Warnings and Invitations," Christ's "Ascension and Reign," "Judgment," "Retribution" and "Heaven" were eliminated (sections on "Original Sin" and "Hell" had been removed from earlier hymnals). New sections included "Kingdom of God," "Service" and "Brotherhood."

3. The subject of redemption was de-emphasized and while formal worship received a new focus. An important symbol of this shift was the replacing of "O For a Thousand Tongues to Sing" (a hymn about redemption) with "Holy, Holy, Holy" as the first hymn in the book. ("O For a Thousand Tongues to Sing" became hymn number 162.)

4. The affirmation of historic Christian doctrines was muted and sometimes revised. A number of references to blood or bleeding were deleted. Wesley's witness to the Virgin Birth in "Hark! the Herald Angels Sing" was changed from:

> *Late in time behold him come,*
> *offspring of the virgin's womb,*

to

> *Long desired, behold him come,*
> *finding here his humble home.*

And because liberals were loath to refer to Jesus Christ as God, the last line in "For the Beauty of the Earth" was changed from:

> *Christ, our God to thee we sing,*

to

> *Lord of all, to thee we raise.*

5. The church's ritual was changed significantly. References to "redeemed by the blood" and learning the Apostles' Creed and the catechism were deleted in the baptismal service. Adults were no longer asked to affirm the Apostles' Creed and to "flee from the devil and his works" in the service of baptism. Two creeds were added, "A Modern Affirmation" and "The Korean Creed," both of which posit a Christianity without a cross.

6. The hymnal committee responded to requests (from the few rather than the many) for hymns about peace and justice and working for one's "fellow man." These hymns, it was believed, would reflect newer understandings of missions, brotherhood and the kingdom of God and would represent the future focus of the church.[1]

Theological revisionism within Methodism had actually begun process long before the 1935 hymnal was published. The hymnal did not introduce reworked Methodist theology as much as it represented the conquest of that theology, at least among official decision-makers in the church.

From the beginning of Methodism in America, there had always been a sociological gap between the more formal, educated and sophisticated Methodism of the cities and the rowdy, revivalistic Methodism of the frontier. The former was symbolized by robed choirs and the official hymnal, while the latter was represented by the gospel quartet and the camp meeting spiritual.

Until the time of the Civil War, Methodism in the cities could have been labeled "conservative" because it honored Methodism's British heritage and was more Anglican in style and substance. During the same period, Methodism on the frontier could have been labeled "liberal" because it was reformist in social outlook and had little regard for tradition, manners and custom.

The Civil War (and other factors) began to change all that. The end of the war and the freeing of the slaves had not brought God's Jubilee. A devastated South and increasing urbanization brought new problems to America. Sin persisted.

As a result, the optimism of evangelical post-millennialism (the belief that the world is getting better and better, leading up to the thousand years of peace after which Christ will return) gave way to the pessimism of evangelical pre-millennialism (the view that the world is getting worse and only Christ's coming to set up his kingdom can save it).

Revivalist Methodism began to retrench and retreat into several forms of what later became known as fundamentalism. Revivalists were attracted especially to the doctrine of holiness and some of its moral teachings (prohibitions against drinking, dancing, card playing and so forth). Musically, the camp meeting spiritual gave way to the Sunday school song which in turn yielded to the gospel hymn. The evangelical movement, once liberal, began to codify itself and feel and act much more conservative.

At the same time establishment Methodism, growing increasingly uncomfortable with the denomination's frontier image, was becoming attracted by the possibilities education and secular wisdom afforded the cause of religion. Some evangelical post-millennialism began to phase into evangelical liberalism. If God's kingdom did not come by revival, perhaps it could come throughout political and social action.

Interest in the emerging disciplines of psychology and sociology began to replace reliance on doctrine and Bible teaching. Musically, the hymns of Wesley began to give way to hymns written by Unitarians and New England liberals which stressed brotherhood and the coming new age.

No one could accuse the Methodist hymnals of 1878, 1889 and 1905 of seriously deviating from orthodoxy, but it is noteworthy that these hymnals were dominated by New England writers, introduced Unitarian hymns, included fewer hymns by Wesley, and de-emphasized doctrines such as Original Sin, hell and Judgment.

The editor of the 1878 hymnal, Richard Wheatley, railed at those in the denomination who did not seem in tune with the tastes and thinking of establishment Methodism.

> Lyrically, or hymnically, the Methodist Episcopal Church is demoralized to an extent that would call down the heartiest denunciation of John Wesley, and of St. Paul too, could they enter upon a fresh tour of episcopal supervision.

This sad state of affairs he laid at the feet of the gospel hymn publishers.

> Pushing publishers, also, competed with the standard manual, and, where successful, not infrequently introduced heterodoxy tenfold more dangerous than all Charles Wesley's lapses put together, besides vitiating the poetical taste of the people.[2]

Methodist's new theology focused on learning: new science, new ideas, a new way of understanding the faith. Its inspiration was the example and teachings of Jesus.

> *O Master, let me walk with thee*
> *in lowly paths of service free.*
> *Tell me thy secret; help me bear*
> *the strain of toil, the fret of care.*
> *(UMH #430)*

This religion taught that if we could follow the footsteps of Jesus and live by the Sermon on the Mount, and persuade the rest of society to join our efforts, religion could realize its goal. That goal was variously stated: the Christianizing of society, bringing the kingdom of God on earth, or living under the Fatherhood of God and the Brotherhood of Man.

Evil, in this system, was not personal sin which required a personal Savior. It was social sin, which could be solved by forming a new society. By 1900 institutional Methodism, once characterized as conservative, was being seen as revisionist and liberal. These Methodists had little interest in conserving historic faith, but they showed great interest in using whatever faith was there, along with secular learning, for the cause of a new social order.

One of the first Methodist hymn writers to express this new emphasis was Frank Mason North.

> *Where cross the crowded ways of life,*
> *where sound the cries of race and clan;*
> *above the noise of selfish strife,*
> *we hear your voice, O Son of man!*
>
> *In haunts of wretchedness and need,*
> *on shadowed thresholds dark with fears,*
> *from paths where hide the lures of greed,*
> *we catch the vision of your tears. (UMH #427)*

It is said that North's hymn was inspired by a walk through Times Square in New York. Written in 1903 as a missionary hymn, it represents the changing emphasis from winning souls to social concerns.

The struggle to remake the denomination during the period from 1890 to 1925 took place on two fronts: the opening to liberal or "modernist" thought on the one hand, and the attempt to cast aside frontier, evangelical, revivalist and holiness influences on the other.

During the 1890s both the North and South Methodist Episcopal Churches sought to distance themselves officially from independent evangelists, holiness associations and the camp meeting movement—all centers of evangelical activity. These institutional pressures led to large scale defections from Methodism and the forming of numerous Holiness-Pentecostal groups from 1890-1910. Many of those who left came from inner cities or poor sections of communities. Ironically the very theology that spoke of concern for the poor disdained the poor people within its own ranks (a situation that persists today).

In Christian education, Sunday school literature began to de-emphasize the concepts of sin, hell, repentance, and conversion, arguing that these were unnecessary topics since all people are children of God by birth.The purpose of Sunday school was no longer to learn Bible stories and doctrine but to instill attitudes, values and responsibility.

By 1920 the ritual of the Methodist Church no longer required new members to respond to the question: "Do you believe in the doctrines of the Holy Scriptures as set forth in the Articles of Religion of the Methodist Episcopal Church?" The baptismal service omitted the phrases, "forasmuch as all men are conceived and born in sin" and "except a man be born of water and the Spirit, he cannot enter the kingdom of God."

By the mid-twenties the modernist take-over of the denomination was nearly complete. Denominational colleges, in their efforts to seek respectability, listed fewer and fewer religious requirements for faculty and students. They were moving from being "Christian" schools to being "church-related" schools. In a few years they would become effectively secularized.

In a study of the theological commitment of Protestant seminaries conducted by *Minister's Monthly*, by 1925 every Methodist seminary of both the southern and northern church considered its orientation to be "modernist." Of all the major denominations, only Methodism could identify none of its seminaries as "orthodox" or "mixed." (United Brethren and Evangelicals combined listed three seminaries as "orthodox.")[3]

Never had a denomination capitulated so totally and so quickly to a foreign ideology as did Methodism. All efforts to pull Methodism back to the historic mainstream failed. The die was cast. On an official denominational level, the church had sold itself to liberalism. The new vision, the new teaching, was considered the wave of the future. Church leaders outdid themselves in their efforts to expound the New Age, the New Man and the New Society. Everything was "new." It was a day of optimism.

> *Lead on, O King eternal,*
> *the day of march has come;*
> *henceforth in fields of conquest*
> *thy tents shall be our home. (UMH #580)*

The mid 1920s was the watershed for Methodism, both theologically and musically. Before that time, Methodists dominated the field of gospel and evangelical music. This did not happen because official Methodism blessed the music, but rather because the Methodist ethos was gospel and evangelical-oriented, and lent itself to that kind of music.

"The Old Rugged Cross" was written by Methodist evangelist George Bennard in 1913. "Great Is Thy Faithfulness" came from another Methodist evangelist, Thomas O. Chisholm, in 1923. Homer Rodeheaver, the Methodist song leader for Billy Sunday in the 1910s and 1920s, popularized hymns such as "I Serve a Risen Savior" and "In the Garden." The great United Brethren publisher, E.S. Lorenz, sometimes known as the dean of American gospel, actively wrote and edited music through the 1920s. Albert Tindley, the Methodist preacher whose music was the forerunner of black gospel, was active into the 1920s.

But after the 1920s, Methodism marched to a different tune.It no longer offered the ethos and inspiration that could spawn gospel and other popular music of the people. Inspiration for such music after the 1920s came from other groups and denominations.

Liberalism focused on a different type of music. The Hymn Society of America came to life in the mid 1920s. While it saw itself as carrying on in the tradition of the great British hymn writers, the society was also committed to hymns for the New Age that reflected the newer views on peace, brotherhood, justice and missions. It wished to raise music above the individualism, privatism and the tasteless, repetitious style of Sunday school music and the gospel hymn. Hymns endorsed by the Hymn Society stressed noble thoughts, beauty, courage, truth, bravery and human responsibility.

> *Rise up, O men of God!*
> *Have done with lesser things.*
> *Give heart and soul and mind and strength*
> *to serve the King of kings. (UMH #576)*

Some of the hymns born of this new ideology have captured our imagination and are favorites today in both liberal and evangelical churches.

> *God of grace and God of glory,*
> *on thy people pour thy power,*
> *crown thine ancient church's story,*
> *bring her bud to glorious flower.*
> *(UMH #577)*

and

> *Joyful, joyful, we adore thee,*
> *God of glory, Lord of love;*
> *hearts unfold like flowers before thee,*
> *opening to the sun above. (UMH #89)*

Other Methodist writers caught up in this new approach to religion contributed hymns such as "Are Ye Able" by Earl Marlatt (UMH #530), "Hope of the World" by Georgia Harkness (UMH #178) and "God of Love and God of Power" by Gerald Kennedy (UMH #578).

Numerous other hymns inspired by modernism and the social gospel poured forth from the pens of authors. They found their way into a myriad of hymn books, including the 1935 and 1966 Methodist hymnals.

In retrospect, however, these hymns as a whole never did capture the hearts and imaginations of the people for whom they were intended, just as the liberal theology on which they were based has been a theology for the few, not the many. In the 1920s, when liberalism was hailed for its relevance to the thinking of the day, it was considered to be the only approach that could save Christianity from the challenge of humanistic skepticism. Various forms of revivalism, literalism and fundamentalism, the liberals argued, would crumble before the onslaughts of modern learning and an increasingly irreligious world.

The same arguments continue to be made today, despite all the evidence to the contrary. At the time of the Civil War, Methodism in America (including the various groups that now comprise the United Methodist Church) was the religion of choice for more than a third of the country. It remained the most influential religious body well into the 1900s. Methodism was evangelical in style and theology and appealed to all classes and types of people.

Sometime in the 1920s, shortly after the denomination passed into the hands of revisionists, the number of Baptist churches surpassed the number of Methodist churches in America. A few years later, in the 1930s, Baptists passed Methodists in membership. One branch of the Baptist Church, the Southern Baptists, surpassed a merged United Methodist denomination in membership in the early 1970s. By the late 1980s Southern Baptists could claim half again as many members as United Methodism, and six times as many foreign missionaries.

In the 1920s, the percentage of Protestants belonging to churches affiliated with the Federal Council of Churches (the predecessor of the National Council of Churches) totaled more than seventy percent of all Protestants. These churches—Episcopalians, Presbyterians, Congregationalists, Methodists and Disciples of Christ—dominated the American religious scene.

By the late 1980s, however, the percentage of Protestants belonging to churches affiliated with the National Council of Churches, the successor to the Federal Council, had fallen to less than fifty percent. What was once known as "mainline" Christianity had become "sideline." The excitement in American church life had passed to more evangelical denominations, parachurch groups, independent ministries and the several Pentecostal and charismatic movements. The denominations that sold themselves into liberalism had, in large part, become not only out-of-touch, but dull.

This does not mean that the United Methodist Church is not still a great denomination with much spiritual vitality. It does suggest, however, that part of the responsibility for Methodism's present situation—a decreasing and aging membership, an inability to reach the masses and lack of a focused mission—must be laid at the feet of the kind of liberal theology that has dominated the church's seminaries, its boards and agencies and much of its official life since the 1920s.

Hymns Inspired by Social Gospel

These conclusions can be confirmed by examining a study of hymns that were inspired by liberalism and the social gospel. A large number of these hymns entered the Methodist hymnals of 1935 and 1966. A few, as noted earlier, are well known today. Large numbers, however, do not appear in *The United Methodist Hymnal* of 1989. Good poetry and good music notwithstanding, they, and the theology they espouse, have not captured the hearts and sentiments of the vast majority of United Methodists. They were not included in the hymnal because they were not being sung.

This study includes all the hymns written in the last one hundred years which appear in the 1935 and 1966 hymnals but which do not appear in the 1989 hymnal.[4]

The study took special note of key ideas, key words and key phrases. A summary of some of the study's findings can be found in chapter fourteen.

What can be said about these hymns? The first thing to note is that the list includes no evangelical or gospel hymns. Almost all the hymns reflect the effort to interpret the new theology for the new age. They might well be labeled, "new words for a new day." They represent liberalism translated into music and worship. (See the word study on these hymns summarized in the table in chapter fourteen.)

Secondly, it should be noted that, when considered separately, none of the hymns is terribly objectionable. The poetry is good, the music uplifting. The emphases sometime serve as correctives to evangelical imbalances. However, when analyzed as a group, these hymns portray a weak and uncertain gospel. To illustrate:

1. One is immediately impressed by the fact that this is Christianity without a cross. There is no atonement. Christ does not die for sin in these hymns; there is no mention of blood or tears or Calvary or Christ as Redeemer. There are only a few references to sin and grace and no mention of hell. Christianity seems reduced to an appeal to God to help us in our human strivings.

2. While these hymns address God in many different ways, most of them do not use the words and images of Scripture but refer to God-in-general, often using "God of . . ." language: "God of love," "God of beauty," "God of the ages," "God of the future," "God of earth and altar," "Lord of interstellar space." References to the second person of the Trinity almost always stress the human rather than the divine nature of Christ. Our Lord is almost never called "Jesus" (the evangelical term of endearment), "Savior" or "Lamb of God." More likely, he is called "Master," "Carpenter," "Man of Galilee" or "Master workman of the race." There are almost no references to the Holy Spirit.

3. Whereas gospel songs and traditional Christianity view the Christian's hope as eternal life, "new words for a new day" hymns espouse Christians' hope in a world that is supposedly getting better and better every day. In this belief, heaven is replaced by a coming kingdom on earth, as described in phrases like "brighter hope," "earth shall be fair," "hasten the perfect day," "nobler life," "kindlier things."

> *At length there dawns the glorious day*
> *by prophets long foretold;*
> *at length the chorus clearer grows*
> *that shepherds heard of old.*
> *The day of dawning brotherhood*
> *breaks on our eager eyes,*
> *and human hatreds flee before*
> *the radiant eastern skies.*
> *(The Book of Hymns, 1966, #189, v. 1)*

4. Like most liberal theology, even today, these hymns blur the distinction between the orders of creation and the orders of redemption. They emphasize the created world rather than Christ's act of redemption on the cross and what that means for today.

These hymns do not mention the Fall or distinguish between what Wesley called "sinners" and "believers." Christ is seen only as an example, and, if his crucifixion is mentioned, it is also as an example. The word "world" is almost always used in a positive sense ("This is my Father's world") rather than in a negative sense ("This world is not my home"). The word "power" is almost always identified with majesty, might and the created world ("When lightnings flash and storm winds blow, There is thy power"). In contrast, evangelical hymns usually associate power with victory over sin ("There is power in the blood") and new life in the Spirit.

5. These hymns emphasize human effort, not the grace of God. One gets the impression from reading them that Christianity has been reduced to girding up the loins, trying harder, working more and doing better. The focus is on "man's" abilities rather than God's grace. An example is hymn #243 in the 1966 hymnal:

> *March on, O soul, with strength!*
> *Like those strong men of old*
> *Who 'gainst enthroned wrong*
> *Stood confident and bold.*

The difference between this theology and evangelical theology is the difference between "Rise Up, O Men of God" and "Amazing Grace."

6. These hymns also downplay and obscure the supernatural elements of Christianity. One does not celebrate the Virgin Birth in these hymns nor God's intervention because of prayer nor

miracles. An effort to interpret Christ's ascension into heaven reads like this in hymn #456 of the 1966 hymnal,

And have the bright immensities
Received our risen Lord,
Where light-years frame the Pleiades
And point Orion's sword?
Do flaming suns his footsteps trace
Through corridors sublime,
The Lord of interstellar space
And conqueror of time?

The heaven that hides him from our sight
Knows neither near nor far:
An altar candle sheds its light
As surely as a star;
And where his loving people meet
To share the gift divine,
There stands he with unhurrying feet;
There heavenly splendors shine.

The hymn suggests we need a much less transcendent and much more imminent Jesus. It implies that we shouldn't think of Jesus as having ascended bodily into heaven, where he sits at the right hand of the Father interceding for us, but as a sort of divine presence surrounding us at all times.

At their best, the hymns that grew out of the liberal reaction to historic faith call us to greater sensitivity to the needs of a hurting world. They urge responsible action on the part of Christ's church. They represent the hopes and dreams of a number of United Methodists.

At their worst, such hymns seem dated. They reflect a theology whose various forms are like so many passing fads. In seeking to be relevant, they bypass the essence of Christianity. They fail to reach "modern man" because of their narrow understanding of who modern man is.

To the credit of the committee that worked on the 1989 United Methodist hymnal, most of these hymns have been deleted.The "new words for the new day" hymns carried over into the new hymnal are those that have gained popular acceptance and which are part of the mainstream of the life of the church today.

To Do

The following are some hymns from the liberal tradition which *The United Methodist Hymnal* retained from earlier hymnals. Respond to the following questions about each hymn:

1. Has this hymn been a part of your United Methodist experience?

2. With what do you associate the hymn? (Church camp? Worship services? Family gatherings?)

3. What feelings does the hymn rouse in you?

"Are Ye Able" (UMH #530)

"O Day of God, Draw Nigh" (UMH #730)

"O Holy City, Seen of John" (UMH #726)

"The Voice of God Is Calling" (UMH #436)

"O Young and Fearless Prophet" (UMH #444)

"Hope of the World"(UMH #178)

"God of Love and God of Power" (UMH #578)

Eight

Evangelical Images

Harold Pusey, a man from one of Union Chapel's well-known families, had died. Two of his brothers were Methodist pastors. There would be a big church funeral and funeral dinner. When I got the news, I began preparing the funeral message in my mind. At seminary we had been discussing the nature of Christian hope: Our faith affirmed the resurrection of the body rather than the immortality of the soul. I decided that would be a good funeral topic, especially with the kind of people who would be attending.

It did not work out that way, however. Brother Raymond, another pastor, was asked to conduct the funeral. I tried to be gracious and understanding. After all, I was only twenty-three years old and had been the pastor at Union Chapel only a few months. Brother Raymond had been close to the family for years.

Brother Raymond was one of the old-timers. I did not label him as such at the time because I was too new to have any impressions about old-timers. But that's how I later identified him. The old-timers were the group I associated with the Sunday morning love feast at annual conference. They would get together to sing old hymns and tell preacher war stories. Most of them were supply pastors and circuit preachers. They had not served the county seat churches and seldom spoke on the conference floor. But they shared a special kind of camaraderie that was a blessing to me, a young pastor.

However, at the time of the funeral Brother Raymond was just another outside preacher to me. His funeral sermon was boring.

The text was from somewhere in Joshua, an extended passage that seemed to go on much too long. The old preacher spent a lot of time talking about the Israelites and their long journey in the wilderness until finally they made it to the River Jordan and how difficult it was to cross Jordan but how happy they were in Canaan.

I was appalled. What a wonderful opportunity to talk about the resurrection of the body. But instead we got bogged down in an obscure Old Testament passage. The family would be sorry they did not have me preach.

But I was wrong. The family, as well as the rest of the congregation, appreciated Brother Raymond's message. Some wept, not because they suffered anguish, but because they were deeply moved. After the trip to the cemetery, church members and family went to the home and thanked God for the message, for Harold Pusey, for Brother Raymond, for the church and for the faith.

I am not sure why, but the funeral and that message stuck in my mind. It perplexed me. Then one day ten or fifteen years later, while driving in my car, I had a moment of insight. I finally understood the sermon and what had happened at the funeral.

The story of the children of Israel is not just a chronicle of the Hebrew covenant people many years ago; it is also a story about Harold Pusey and the rest of us. The journey through the wilderness is Harold's journey and our journey. We wander in desert lands, but God leads us.

> *Guide me, O thou great Jehovah,*
> *pilgrim through this barren land.*
> *I am weak, but thou art mighty;*
> *hold me with thy powerful hand.*
> *(UMH #127)*

The Jordan River is the last barrier to Canaan, the promised land.

> *When I tread the verge of Jordan,*
> *bid my anxious fears subside;*
> *death of death and hell's destruction,*
> *land me safe on Canaan's side.*

The people of Union Chapel had lived with those images and that language for years. It was part of their heritage. No one had to explain it to them. They understood.

But I, caught up in the philosophy and theology of seminary, with its rational explanations and critical approach to the Bible, had not understood. What had seemed dull to me had struck a deep spiritual chord in the hearts of those people. I realize now that the sermon I had prepared in my mind (and probably preached on other occasions), a theologically orthodox and well-reasoned argument for the resurrection of the body, was far less appropriate for Harold Pusey's funeral than Brother Raymond's account of the journey through the wilderness.

In our world, one can possess a lot of knowledge, even about spiritual things, but have limited spiritual understanding. This is the truth the apostle Paul explained to the Corinthian people.

> This is what we speak, not in words taught us by human wisdom but in words taught by the Spirit, expressing spiritual truths in spiritual words. The man without the Spirit does not accept the things that come from the Spirit of God, for they are foolishness to him, and he cannot understand them, because they are spiritually discerned (1 Corinthians 2:13-14).

For Christians, spiritual truths are based on God's self-revelation in the Scriptures. Scripture stories are told and retold, interpreted, expanded and celebrated by believers in worship, music and teaching. Since we are part of that great story, our own spiritual stories are also told and celebrated within the community of believers. The truths we express are different from the "truths" of the non-believing world. Therefore, symbols, images and language we use in our faith walk differs from our conversation in the everyday world.

To put it another way, we share a way of speaking and imagining with television script writers and gas station attendants. It is desacralized, public schoolroom language in which words like sin, miracles and salvation carry secular meanings. We use this language to shop at the grocery store, study chemistry and talk about the weather. It is the language of the world, and while believers use it for everyday discourse, it is not our "native" tongue, for we are, after all, pilgrims in this barren land.

Our native tongue is faith language, the language of the sermon, prayer and hymn book. It is undemythologized language about cleansed souls, the Lamb of God and the hill of Calvary. Its

King James sound and its unabashed supernaturalism make it embarrassing to sanitized, McGraw-Hill types. However, to common, ordinary believers, it is the Christian family language. We use it to marry and bury, confess our sins and hope for eternal life.

We also use this language to express our understanding of how the world really is. This is important because this view of reality, or truth, sets the Christian apart. The secular world likes to reserve for itself the right to define "truth," and it usually does so with an appeal to what can be seen, heard and otherwise observed and proven. Religion, according to this view, might help persons find a reason for living, choose life values or cope with problems, but psychology, education or art might be just as helpful. Religion, this view contends, does not deal with objective truth.

But we are not Christians simply because it makes us feel better or allows us to cope with problems. We are Christians because Christianity is true, not just subjectively true (true for me while something else may be true for someone else) but objectively true. That is, there is a God who did create the world. This God has a plan for the world which includes the coming of Jesus Christ, his death on the cross as an atonement for sin, his resurrection and his coming again.

At the same time, we realize we see this truth as "but a poor reflection as in a mirror" (1 Corinthians 13:12). We are speaking of transcendent reality that is not easily explained in everyday language or even in the specialized language of the philosopher. How, for example, do we speak of heaven, the Second Coming or even God himself? Are we not speaking of the truth in another dimension, on a different level?

It is like trying to describe "red" to blind persons. People who cannot see could deny there is such a thing as "red" because they cannot hear, feel or experience redness. But they may also be convinced a world of sight exists and may be open to our efforts to communicate the idea of redness. To do so, we would have to resort to metaphors and poetry. Red is like brightness . . . or beauty . . . or warmth.

We are similarly limited in understanding and communicating spiritual truth—truth about God, sin and salvation. When we read something like the book of Revelation, we realize that God's real world, the reality beyond the pictures, exceeds any rational explanation.

Because of this, we speak in images. We tell stories. We draw pictures. We use a language that speaks to heart as well as head, one that grows out of our immersion in God's Word. For example, some of the most familiar words in all Scripture are these:

> *The Lord is my shepherd,*
> *I shall not be in want.*

I might attempt to "explain" Psalm 23 with an intellectual discussion of sheep and shepherds, green pastures, valleys of the shadow of death and overrunning cups. That might help me appreciate the psalm, but the truth of the psalm is much deeper than the rational understanding of it. In the psalm's pictures and images, I sense eternal truth: There is a God who loves and cares for me.

When we use the hymnal, we need to have a sense of the images and language that have informed our evangelical past. Following are several examples of these for consideration:

Pilgrim Through this Barren Land

> *On Jordan's stormy banks I stand,*
> *and cast a wishful eye*
> *to Canaan's fair and happy land,*
> *where my possessions lie. (UMH #724)*

The people from Union Chapel who heard Brother Raymond's funeral sermon responded to a theme common in evangelical hymnody—whether from Wesley or the camp meetings, Negro spirituals or southern gospel. The Christian life is a pilgrimage which starts as escape from Egypt through the Red Sea, continues as a wandering through the wilderness to Jordan, with Canaan, or heaven, as the final destination.

> *From Egypt lately freed*
> *by the Redeemer's grace,*
> *a rough and thorny path we tread*
> *in hopes to see his face.*
> *Chorus: Hallelujah!*
> *We're on our way home.*
> (Early camp meeting spiritual)

This theme is most graphically expressed in camp meeting music. The poetry of the camp meeting spirituals was never great by the canons of literature, but it was always vivid. In early camp meeting songsters (especially before 1850), "pilgrim" is one of the most frequently used words identifying the believer:

> *I'm a pilgrim and a stranger passing o'er,*
> *the road may be rough, but 'tis clear,*
> *and a starry crown awaits me o'er the river,*
> *and Jesus bids me welcome there.*
> *(The Revivalist #573)*

Sometimes the journey is pleasant:

> *How happy is the pilgrim's lot,*
> *I'm on my way to Zion.*
> *How free from ev'ry anxious thought,*
> *I'm on my way to Zion.*
> (Early camp meeting chorus)

Sometimes the journey is full of trials:

> *Gwine to write to Massa Jesus,*
> *to send some valiant soldier,*
> *to turn back Pharaoh's army,*
> *Hallelu! to turn back Pharaoh's army.*
> *I'm a rolling,*
> *I'm a rolling,*
> *I'm a rolling through an unfriendly world.*
> (Negro spiritual)

The fact that so many of these early Methodist songs mention hardship and trial reveals the extent to which frontier Methodism was a movement of the poor. For blacks, the hardship was suffering under slavery; Pharaoh's army was the slavery system from which God's people needed deliverance.

At the end of the journey was death, the River Jordan:

> *I looked over Jordan, and what did I see,*
> *coming for to carry me home?*
> *A band of angels coming after me,*
> *coming for to carry me home.*
> *(UMH #703)*

Because our circumstances have changed, the pilgrim theme may not be as integral a part of our spiritual lives as it was for our Methodist forebears. For those of us immersed in Scripture, hymnody and the symbols of our tradition, however, the image still powerfully tugs at our hearts.

> *I am bound for the promised land,*
> *I am bound for the promised land,*
> *O who will come and go with me?*
> *I am bound for the promised land.*
> *(UMH #724)*

Coming Home

> *Come, ye thankful people, come,*
> *raise the song of harvest home;*
> *all is safely gathered in,*
> *e're the winter storms begin. . . .*
> *Even so, Lord, quickly come,*
> *bring thy final harvest home;*
> *gather thou thy people in,*
> *free from sorrow, free from sin.*
> *(UMH #694)*

The hymn "Come, Ye Thankful People, Come" is usually associated with Thanksgiving. Based on the parable in Mark 4:26-29, the hymn actually uses a harvest theme to illustrate God's judgment and the second coming of Christ. The hymn uses another image, "home," as the place of abode for the believer.

The word "home" appears only occasionally in most translations of the Bible, although the word "family" is used frequently, as is the word "house." The fascination with home in Christian imagery is based in part on verses such as Hebrews 3:6 and Luke 14:16-24. Home is the Father's house, the place where we belong, the place of love.

An even greater inspiration in the evangelical tradition is the image of home that comes from the story of the Prodigal Son (Luke 15:11-32). This is perhaps the most popular of all the Methodist revival texts. A number of invitation hymns use the home theme.

> *Come home, come home,*
> *you who are weary, come home;*
> *earnestly, tenderly, Jesus is calling,*

> *calling, O sinner, come home!*
> *(UMH #348)*

> *Come, O my guilty brethren, come,*
> *groaning beneath your load of sin;*
> *his bleeding heart shall make you room,*
> *his open side shall take you in.*
> *He calls you now, invites you home:*
> *come, O my guilty brethren, come.*
> *(UMH #342)*

"Home" is an image used for salvation, peace and security (in God's presence)—and for heaven.

In many hymns, the home theme is related to the pilgrim theme. Home is the final destiny for the pilgrim, the heaven that is beyond the river death.

> *Deep, deep river,*
> *my home is over Jordan;*
> *deep, deep river, Lord,*
> *I want to cross over into campground.*
> (Familiar Negro spiritual)

Zion

Related to pilgrim and home imagery, and yet different, is the symbol "Zion."

> *Glorious things of thee are spoken,*
> *Zion, city of our God. (UMH #731)*

In the evangelical tradition, "Zion" generally refers to the church, or to churches. We use it to name churches (Zion United Methodist Church), church publications (*Zion's Herald*) and denominations (African Methodist Episcopal Church, Zion). We also use it to name the people of God, or the church universal.

> *'Tis the old ship of Zion,*
> *get on board, get on board.*
> *(UMH #345)*

"Zion" is an example of a word whose poetic layers can be studied in Scripture. Originally Zion was the name of the hill on which the city of Jerusalem (later known as the City of David—see 2 Samuel 5:7) stood. It then became a synonym for Jerusalem

(Isaiah 52:1) and for the people who lived in Jerusalem (Lamentations 1:17). And since Jerusalem was the capital of the nation, Zion came to mean not only the people who lived in the city but all of Israel (Psalm 132:13).

When Jerusalem became a holy place (because of the temple), Zion was also used to indicate the dwelling place of God and the source of blessing.

> *The hill of Zion yields*
> *a thousand sacred sweets*
> *before we reach the heavenly fields,*
> *or walk the golden streets.*
> *(UMH #733)*

Then, in addition, because God dwelt in his people, Zion was used to refer to the holy people, or the people who belong to God (Isaiah 52:6-7).

In the New Testament, the church (or Zion) inherited the promises (and the symbols) of the people of God, so that the church in Revelation 21:2 is called the Holy City or new Jerusalem. In this usage, Zion means not only the church but also the place that God has prepared for his people—in other words, heaven (Hebrews 12:22).

With such rich imagery in Scripture itself, is it any wonder that Zion has so many meanings in our hymnody?

> *O Zion, haste, thy mission high fulfilling,*
> *to tell to all the world that God is light.*
> *(UMH #573)*

> *We're marching to Zion,*
> *beautiful, beautiful Zion;*
> *we're marching upward to Zion,*
> *the beautiful city of God.*
> *(UMH #733)*

A Fountain Filled with Blood

Perhaps the most powerful image in the evangelical heritage is that of the blood of Jesus. In hymnody, the blood is sprinkled, poured and shed. It flows in waves, fountains, lakes and streams. It washes, cleanses, purifies, atones, redeems, purchases and effects. In more liturgical settings, it is our drink. It sustains. In evangelical settings, the blood effects forgiveness of sins and brings peace, healing and wholeness. Behind the image is God's self-giving love through the cross to make right in the world what has been made wrong by sin.

> *There is a fountain filled with blood*
> *drawn from Immanuel's veins;*
> *and sinners, plunged beneath that flood,*
> *lose all their guilty stains.*
> *(UMH #622)*

Behind the song's imagery is the thought that if God's cost in the salvation process is the cross, so that God's grace becomes available through the self-giving sacrifice of Christ, and the symbol for that is blood, then the amount of grace (blood) that is available is not a drop nor a sprinkle, but a fountain, a stream or a sea. It is more than we could hope to imagine.

> *And can it be that I should gain*
> *an interest in the Savior's blood!*
> *(UMH #363)*

Perhaps no other hymn writer used blood imagery as frequently as Charles Wesley (see chapter fourteen). In Wesleyan theology, the blood of Jesus makes possible prevenient grace, justifying grace and sanctifying grace.

> *I felt my Lord's atoning blood*
> *close to my soul applied;*
> *me, me he loved, the Son of God,*
> *for me, for me he died!*
> *(UMH #58)*

This emphasis of the Wesleys became central in early American Methodist preaching and singing.

> *What can wash away my sin?*
> *Nothing but the blood of Jesus.*
> *What can make me whole again?*
> *Nothing but the blood of Jesus.*
> *(UMH #362)*

Though written by a Baptist (Robert Lowry), "What Can Wash Away My Sin?" can be traced to the Methodist campgrounds at

Ocean Grove, New Jersey. The song was introduced there and became so popular that, according to one commentator, it was sometimes used in the services as the prelude, the offertory, the hymn of praise and frequently as the invitation hymn.

The use of blood imagery has not been without critics.

Liberal theology, which posits the concept of grace without atonement, is uncomfortable with the idea that only in the cross is salvation (and grace) possible. And since the Atonement is one of the dividing marks between various forms of liberalism and historic orthodox theology, "the blood" becomes a theological issue. For this reason, persons have expressed concern lest the new hymnal "take out the blood." However, there is considerably more blood imagery in the 1989 United Methodist hymnal than in the two previous official Methodist hymnals.

Other questions about blood imagery have to do with the kind of metaphors that communicate effectively to the modern mind. Some argue that the picture of blood is messy and uncouth and in poor taste. People do not think in such primitive concepts any more. In an educated world among respectable people there should be different and new ways to communicate Christian truth.

But references to blood in Christianity are not that easily discarded. The word blood appears in Scripture nearly 350 times, almost always in the context of grace, guilt, expiation, covenant, forgiveness and peace. It is so integral to the idea of the cross and the sacraments that efforts to "update" the imagery have often merely de-emphasized the central truths of Christianity. In the last analysis, it is difficult to improve on the images and emphases of Scripture and our Methodist heritage.

> *The blood that Jesus shed for me,*
> *way back on Calvary,*
> *the blood that gives me strength from day to day,*
> *it will never lose its power.*
> (Andre Crouch, contemporary gospel hymn)

To Do

1. Many images, pictures and symbols are a part of our faith language. Share what you feel and what you think of when you hear the following words or phrases:

A. *The garden*

"I Come to the Garden Alone" (UMH #314)

"I'll Go With Him Through the Garden" (UMH #338)

B. Calvary

"On Calvary" in "I Heard an Old, Old Story" (UMH #370)

"Yonder on Calvary" in "Marvelous Grace of Our Loving Lord" (UMH #365)

C. Glory

"Mine Eyes Have Seen the Glory" (UMH #717)

"Sing With All the Saints in Glory" (UMH #702)

2. The 1989 United Methodist hymnal has attempted to introduce some new images to our faith language and our faith thinking. Share what you feel and think when you hear the following:

A. Wellspring of wisdom

"Wellspring of Wisdom" (UMH #506)

B. Web and loom of love

"God of Many Names" (UMH #105)

C. Love's cosmic mind

"How Can We Name a Love?" (UMH #111)

Nine

The Black Perspective

The year was 1875. The place, London. The Moody-Sankey evangelistic crusade was underway at the Haymarket Opera House. On the stage stood the Fisk Jubilee Singers, a group of eleven black students from Fisk University in Nashville, who were in England on tour to raise funds for the university.

But on this occasion, the group of emancipated slaves was not singing for money, nor were they in concert. They were singing for the altar call.

Steal away, steal away,
steal away to Jesus. (UMH #704)

The singers shared a kind of music people had never heard before—Negro spirituals. These were songs about fleeing Pharaoh's land, riding chariots and crossing Jordan, wearing shoes in heaven and gathering at the old campground.

The crowd wept. Sinners were converted.

For several weeks, the singers declined all invitations for concerts to help with the crusade. The crowds were so great that even after Moody and Sankey left to fulfill commitments in other cities the services continued with the Jubilee Singers and several local pastors. Many nights saw ten to twelve thousand people in attendance.

The story of the Fisk Jubilee Singers must be told whenever Negro spirituals or black gospel music is discussed. Fisk University, an effort of the American Missionary Association to educate former slaves, was struggling for funds. Eleven students ventured out by faith, entering unknown and often hostile territory to sing the songs passed on to them from slave plantations and camp meetings.

The students were both widely acclaimed and hissed. They sang before the queen of England and the president of the United States, but they were turned away from inns and made to feel unwelcome in churches. Their goal was to raise money for their school, but their concerts had a powerful religious impact on the hearts and minds of those who listened. And as a quite unintended by-product of their efforts, they introduced the Negro spiritual, the basic form from which much of black music flows to a large part of the world.

Despite the popularity of the Fisk Jubilee Singers and similar groups who came after them, it has taken a long time to recognize the important influence of Negro spirituals and black music on denominational hymnody. While Negro spirituals appeared in independent evangelical hymnals, in the Cokesbury hymnal, in choral arrangements and in camp music, not until the 1966 Methodist hymnal included seven spirituals was this music "blessed" for congregational singing in formal worship.

Now, however, *The United Methodist Hymnal* includes fifty spirituals and gospel hymns from the black perspective, including at least five of the original 128 spirituals from the Fisk Jubilee repertoire ("Deep River," "Go Down, Moses," "My Lord, What a Morning," "'Tis the Old Ship of Zion" and "Nobody Knows the Trouble I've Seen"). This inclusion acknowledges the deep impression this music made on the developing United Methodist ethos, worship and theology.

In addition to music from the black tradition, *The United Methodist Hymnal* also includes music from Hispanic and Asian-American sources and from several nationalities. Thus the hymnal is perhaps the most ethnically inclusive major hymnal on the market today. Most of this music appears in the hymnal to allow United Methodists of various ethnic backgrounds to appreciate other cultures and nationalities. However, music from the black tradition is different. Its development is intrinsically linked with the development of Methodism itself and represents an important chapter in the story of who United Methodists are as a people.

Blacks first arrived in America in 1619. Not nearly enough is known about black life in America for the next two hundred years, particularly black religious life. We know little about the heroes, the leaders and the saints. Most blacks were slaves, but many were not (about ten percent of all blacks were free in 1800). Among Methodists there are accounts of the unheralded Aunt Annie, a slave who was one of the first Methodist converts in the 1760s; Richard Allen, who left the Methodist Church in 1792 and later founded the African Methodist Episcopal Church; and Harry Hosier, evangelist and traveling partner of Francis Asbury. But our information is sketchy.

We do know that the first wholesale acceptance of Christianity by blacks took place after the Revolutionary War and is linked with the same revival that launched Methodism in America. The Methodist message of free grace was readily received by slaves as well as others who were devalued by society. That message emphasized that Christ died for all; therefore any person—rich or poor, male or female, slave or free—could be saved. This bestowed essential worth on all people, including slaves. A soul for whom Christ died was a soul worth saving, somebody created to be a child of God was meant to be a sister or brother in Jesus and to wear the white robes of heaven.

Furthermore, the Methodists proclaimed that religion could be experienced—in other words, felt. This religion was in the heart, the feet and the hands. It could be expressed by crying, laughing, shouting, clapping and even dancing (though it was never called "dancing"). Most importantly, it could be expressed by singing.

Blacks had a reputation for singing even before the Revolutionary War, when their music was often associated with the hymns of Isaac Watts. Reverend Wright of Cumberland County, Virginia, wrote in 1761,

> My Landlord tells me ... they heard the *Slaves* at worship in their lodge, singing Psalms and Hymns in the evening, and again in the morning, long before break of day. They are excellent singers, and long to get some of *Dr. Watts's Psalms* and *Hymns*.[1]

Isaac Watts' imagery is rich in references to heaven, judgment, angels and glory—themes frequently found in Negro spirituals.

The earliest black hymnal, Richard Allen's 1801 book, *A Collection of Spiritual Songs and Hymns,* drew heavily on Watts and Wesley. The type of hymns selected for that hymnal is significant. Wesley's hymn,

> *Father, I stretch my hands to thee;*
> *no other help I know:*
> *if thou withdraw thyself from me,*
> *Ah! whither shall I go?*

was an early favorite, frequently "lined out" (the leader gives a line and the congregation repeats it) and has what would later be known as a blues theme. Watt's hymn,

> *Behold, the awful trumpet sounds,*
> *The sleeping dead to raise.*
> *And calls the nations underground:*
> *O how the saints will praise.*
>
> *The falling stars their orbits leave,*
> *The sun in darkness hide;*
> *The elements asunder cleave,*
> *The moon turn'd into blood.*

was very likely the basis for what the improvisors eventually ended up with in the spiritual, "My Lord, What a Mourning" (changed by those who shy away from judgment imagery to "My Lord, What a Morning" UMH #719).

But the Methodist camp meeting that really opened the door to the development of black music. Blacks flocked to camp meetings in large numbers, and the eyewitness accounts of their presence almost always describe their music. Black choirs outsang white choirs. Blacks sang all night. Black singing reduced sinners to tears and brought great joy to believers.

What blacks brought to the music was the suffering of slavery and the rituals and rhythms of their African past. The camp meeting was a setting away from the restricting hand of the slaveholder, offering fellowship with other blacks and mingling with whites. The setting and the experience itself was uninhibiting and affirming. Camp meetings were known for hand-claps and ring shouts, swaying and moaning, with whites as caught up in the Spirit as blacks.

The results were not without criticism. One "formal" Methodist, Reverend John Watson, wrote in 1819,

> We have too, a growing evil, in the practice of singing in our places of . . . worship, *merry* airs, adapted from old *songs,* to hymns of our composing: often miserable as poetry and senseless as matter. . . . Most frequently composed and first sung by the illiterate *blacks* of the society. . . . In the *blacks'* quarter [of a camp meeting], the coloured people get together, and sing for hours together, short scraps of disjointed affirmations, pledges, or prayers, lengthened out with long repetition *choruses.*[2]

Something new was evolving, part English, part African, not bound by any of the rules of acceptable music, with choruses added before, after or in the middle of verses. It was music without instrumental accompaniment, not committed to paper, not identified by origin, not confined to any recognized meter and not even limited to a customary seven-note scale (often using the traditional African pentatonic or five-note scale).

The music's language and images were based on the Bible, and the themes were biblical, but with layers of meaning. Black spirituals fused all the experiences of life, moving easily between references to suffering, slavery, Satan, the slaveholder, salvation and saints in heaven.

Originally, as sung by slaves, a spiritual like "Steal Away" was very possibly a veiled reference to escaping North. At the same time, it may have been a guarded invitation to slip away to prohibited church services or perhaps a longing for death and the peace that would come from being with Jesus.

The references to slavery and freedom from slavery are very apparent in a spiritual such as "Go Down, Moses" (UMH #448):

> *When Israel was in Egypt's land,*
> *let my people go;*
> *oppressed so hard they could not stand,*
> *let my people go.*

The Fisk Jubilee Singers' version of this spiritual has twenty-five verses. It links "Israel" with slaves, "Egypt" with the South and the system of slavery, "Pharaoh" with slaveowners and oppressors, "crossing the Red Sea" with emancipation, the "wilderness" with life beyond slavery and "Canaan" with heaven. For good measure, it also contains one verse that shows the Methodist influence on the spiritual:

> *I'll tell you what I likes de best,*
> *let my people go;*
> *it is the shouting Methodist,*
> *let my people go.*

This reference to "Methodist" focuses on a matter that is seldom recognized when Negro spirituals are discussed, and that is the close tie between many spirituals and their images with Methodist frontier religion. As early as 1797, Francis Asbury used a metaphor from a spiritual when he spoke of the "Egypt of South Carolina" in a reference to Africans and the South.[3]

In the original 128 spirituals linked with the Fisk Jubilee Singers,[4] five have direct mention of "Methodist":

> *I'm a Methodist bred and a Methodist born,*
> *there's a meeting here tonight;*
> *And when I'm dead there's a Methodist gone,*
> *there's a meeting here tonight.*

Some of their other spirituals are full of Methodist family language. The well-known spiritual "Mary and Martha" has the line,

> *Crying free grace and dying love,*
> *free grace and dying love,*
> *free grace and dying love,*
> *to ring those charming bells.*

"Free grace" is Methodist code language (see chapter thirteen). Derived from the doctrine of unlimited atonement, it teaches that all persons can be saved. It was the banner under which Methodists marched. This doctrine made Methodists different from Baptists, Congregationalists and other denominational groups.

Linked to the doctrine of free grace is the Methodist tendency to make direct appeals to "sinners," those outside the saving grace of Christ, and "mourners," those longing for and seeking salvation.

> *Oh, sinners, don't stay away,*
> *for the angels say there's room enough,*

room enough in the Heavens for you.

When I was a mourner just like you,
washed in the blood of the Lamb,
I mourned and prayed 'till I got through,
washed in the blood of the Lamb.

Other uniquely Methodist phrases found in spirituals are words such as "backsliding" and "love feast." Because of their belief in predestination and "eternal security," Baptists and other Calvinists did not use the term "backsliding"—it is another Methodist family word.

There's no backsliding in the heaven, my Lord,
how I long to go there too.
Judgment, Judgment, Judgment day is rolling around.

There's a love feast in heaven by and by, children,
Oh! run up, children, get your crown,
there's a love feast in heaven by and by.

The denominational and doctrinal references in the spirituals are not all Methodist by any means. There are also references to "Baptist 'till I die" and "gathering down by the river" (which is understood to be Baptist language). Both Methodists and Baptists were enriched by the revival among blacks.

Before the Civil War, no distinction was made between "spirituals," the general term used for the folk music identified with camp meetings and revivals, and "Negro spirituals," a variant of the camp meeting spiritual that was associated more frequently with blacks and included the images of slavery. Songbooks like *The Revivalist* contain the various kinds of spirituals side by side.

About the time of the Civil War, however, such distinctions were being made and became firmly fixed with the introduction of printed collections and groups such as the Fisk Jubilee Singers. In the hands of people like William Bradbury and Ira Sankey, "spirituals" in mostly white gatherings adopted the developing style of Sunday school and gospel music.

In black churches and black gatherings, the spiritual became more and more entwined with the unique experiences and culture of black people. The music and style identified the singers not just as believers, but as black believers bearing the sufferings and hopes of their African and slavery past.

Negro spirituals and other forms of black music, are much more complex than they appear on the printed page. There is "Swing Low, Sweet Chariot" as it might be sung from the hymnbook. Then there is "Swing Low, Sweet Chariot" as it might be done in a black church, which, if the words were printed, could look something like this:

> *Oh swing low, oh swing low,*
> *Oh swing low, sweet chariot, swing low.*
> *Oh swing low, oh swing low.*
> *Oh swing low sweet chariot, swing low.*
> *It must be Jesus passing by;*
> *Oh swing low sweet chariot, swing low.*
> *Swing low in the East,*
> *Swing low,*
> *Swing low in the West,*
> *Swing low,*
> *Swing low in the East,*
> *Swing low,*
> *Swing low sweet chariot, swing low.*

Originally such a spiritual would have been sung without harmonization, without keyboard or chording instrument and embellished with improvisations. Spirituals were not merely an aid to religious expression, they *were* the religious expression. A spiritual was not a thirty-second chorus or a three-minute hymn, but an act of worship that might last five or ten or fifteen minutes.

For this and other reasons, the Negro spiritual was not always appreciated by more formal and institutionalized Christians. Along with its musical cousins, the camp meeting spiritual and the gospel hymn, the Negro spiritual was criticized for straying outside the bounds of good taste. Its theology seemed simplistic and its style irreverent. One clergyman's comment in 1863 was typical:

> We have heard these (spirituals) long enough, and we hope the good taste of the refined ladies at Port Royal will substitute others more sensible and elevated in language. . . . Let us now endeavor to teach them something better. Here is a specimen which should not be tolerated in these schools:

In the mornin' when I rise
Tell my Jesus, Huddy oh?

We hope the days will come when all such illiterate, we will not say senseless songs, will be discouraged by all who wish and are laboring for the true enlightenment of the African race.[5]

Spirituals and black music were criticized for replacing "standard" hymns; for having texts that were not lyric poems in the hallowed tradition of Watts and Wesley but isolated lines from prayers and Scripture and other hymns; for repeating continuously and being lengthened by choruses and refrains; and for sounding suspiciously like dance tunes and other secular music. This was the same type of criticism leveled against all gospel music.

This reproach continued well into the twentieth century. Many of us who were in seminary in the 1950s remember the sentiments expressed by worship and music leaders of that time: An increasingly sophisticated culture responded to "objective" rather than "subjective" worship. Modern religion should be quiet, reverent and rational. The emotionalism of "holy-roller" churches (which was Methodism's own past) or "hoot-and-holler" churches (referring to black churches) was disdained.

It is unfortunate that the very movement—Methodism—that had helped to spawn the Negro spiritual had become less than hospitable to the music and the kind of religion the music represented well into the twentieth century. It took events of the 1960s to reverse the trend.

By then, however, the damage had been done. Although Methodism established a number of black colleges after the Civil War, developed missionary and social work among blacks, assumed liberal and reformist stances socially and, in more recent years, adopted a missional priority that was supposed to have strengthened the ethnic minority local church, the percentage of Methodists who are black has steadily decreased for a number of years.

In 1800, only about four to five percent of all blacks were listed as church members (a higher percentage may have been believers, but were not official members). As the revival spread, that percentage doubled and tripled and quadrupled. Methodism was particularly enriched by the influx of black members. Within the first couple of decades of the 1800s, approximately twenty percent of all Methodists were black. During this period Methodism had the greatest influence on Negro spirituals.

While the Methodist message and the frontier revival brought many blacks to Methodism, discrimination led to defections by a number of newly formed black Methodist groups.

The first of these new groups was the African Methodist Episcopal Church (AME), led by Richard Allen in 1816. This was followed by the formation of the African Methodist Episcopal Church Zion (AME Zion) in 1821 and the Colored Methodist Episcopal Church (CME) following the Civil War. Another wave of blacks left to join holiness and Pentecostal churches at the turn of the twentieth century.

Other blacks were attracted to the greater congregational freedom that was found among Baptists. In 1800, blacks were equally divided between Methodists and Baptists (no other denominations were successful in winning large numbers of blacks at that time). By 1900, however, the Baptist share of black church members was sixty-seven percent, while the percentage of blacks who were related to the several Methodist groups had dropped to twenty-five percent. The rest were in other denominations.

Nevertheless, Methodism was still the denomination of choice by many black Christians. At the time of World War I, nearly nine percent (320,000) of the 3.7 million members of the Methodist Episcopal Church were black. One of these members was a preacher and camp meeting singer named Charles Albert Tindley (1859-1933). He laid the foundation for what was later known as black gospel.

Tindley founded the East Calvary M.E. Church in Philadelphia (renamed Tindley Temple in 1924) and began to introduce music that combined camp meeting spirituals, Negro spirituals, blues and Ira Sankey gospel. Tindley called his music "evangelistic songs," and, being sensitive to the critics of such music in the M.E. Church, insisted they were not meant for formal, Sunday morning worship—a qualification that was ignored in most black churches and a number of white ones.

Oh by and by, when the morning comes,
when the saints of God are gathered home,
we'll tell the story how we've overcome,

for we'll understand it better by and by.
(UMH #525)

Another Tindley song,

I'll overcome, I'll overcome, I'll overcome some day,
If in my life I do not yield,
I'll overcome some day.

was easily adapted to the civil rights song, "We Shall Overcome" (UMH #533). Another Tindley hymn in the hymnal is "When the Storms of Life are Raging" (UMH #512).

Unfortunately, Tindley music, and later black gospel, were not widely accepted by white, liberal Methodists of the 1920s, 30s, 40s and 50s. Methodist, United Brethren and Evangelical Church hymnals of that period included no Tindley music (and almost no spirituals). Among whites, Tindley's music was better known in evangelical and Pentecostal churches than among the more formal mainline churches.

For this and other reasons the number of blacks within Methodism had decreased dramatically since Tindley. Today, only 3.8% of United Methodists are black. Despite United Methodism's declared commitment to liberal theology and social policy, or perhaps because of it, the United Methodist Church since 1968 has lost 140,000 black members. The image of the denomination is white-dominated, sophisticated, liberal, highly bureaucratic and formal, has not been conducive to attracting large numbers of ethnic minorities to United Methodist Christianity.

Perhaps the inclusion of about fifty spirituals, black gospel and other hymns from the black perspective in the new United Methodist hymnal will help to reverse this trend. These hymns will enrich the worship of all United Methodist churches and testify to the importance of music from the black perspective in the United Methodist tradition.

Two other authors should be mentioned in any discussion of Methodism and music from the black perspective. Thomas Dorsey (1899-1965), usually called the father of (black) gospel music, took the style that Tindley had introduced and added the melodic and harmonic patterns of the blues. Thus he created a kind of music, or perhaps, more accurately, a way of doing music, that characterizes much of black worship today.

Besides his indebtedness to Tindley, Dorsey was also moved by the music of another Methodist, Homer Rodeheaver. He often referred to the power of the singing at a Billy Sunday-Homer Rodeheaver revival in 1911 and its effect on him. Rodeheaver music ("Brighten the Corner Where You Are," "His Eye Is On the Sparrow," "Let the Lower Lights Be Burning," "The Old Rugged Cross") became very popular among blacks. At the same time, many of the Rodeheaver gospel music collections included Negro spirituals.

Dorsey was known in vaudeville and jazz and blues circles, but the church songs of black people exerted a greater and greater pull on his life. Finally, he committed himself totally to the composing and performing of what he called the "gospel song." He popularized the use of the piano (groups that sang Negro spirituals sang a cappella), female soloists (Mahalia Jackson was the best known) and singing groups.

Dorsey's music (such as "There Will Be Peace in the Valley") was for years better known in Pentecostal and holiness churches (both black and white) than in mainline denominations. His best known song, "Precious Lord, Take My Hand"(UMH #474), was written in 1932 during the Depression at a time of deep sorrow. Dorsey had been on tour when he received word that both his wife and his child had died. "Precious Lord" became not only Thomas Dorsey's personal prayer in a time of grief, but also the prayer of a people (and beyond—it has been translated into fifty different languages). It was requested the night of Martin Luther King's death and sung by Mahalia Jackson at his funeral.

The other black composer who should be mentioned is Andre Crouch. Crouch learned piano in his father's holiness church. He became a composer and singer for white as well as black circles (and often alters his concerts depending on which group predominates in the audience). Two of his songs are in the new United Methodist hymnal: "Through It All" (UMH #507) and "To God Be the Glory," also known as "My Tribute" (UMH #99).

To Do

1. In some places (including *The United Methodist Hymnal*), songs traditionally known as Negro spirituals are today being referred to as "Afro-American" spirituals. How many of the fol-

lowing Afro-American spirituals do you know? What is your first remembrance of the spiritual? What feelings or images do you associate with the song?

"We Are Climbing Jacob's Ladder" (UMH #418)
"Do Lord" (UMH #527)
"Nobody Knows the Trouble I've Seen" (UMH #520)
"Swing Low, Sweet Chariot" (UMH #703)
"This Little Light of Mine" (UMH #585)

2. What are the following Afro-American spirituals really about? What did they mean for the original singers? What do they mean for us today?

"I Am Leaning on the Lord" (UMH #416)
"'Tis the Old Ship of Zion" (UMH #345)
"Fix Me" (UMH #655)
"O Mary, Don't You Weep" (UMH #134)
"My Lord, What a Morning" (UMH #719)
"We Are Climbing Jacob's Ladder" (UMH #418)

3. Discuss the meaning of the following images or figures: the Old Ship of Zion, the wilderness, the nations underground, "when you come out," the long white robe, "put on my shoes," "Pharaoh's army got drowned."

Ten

Women's Images

Those who have followed the development of *The United Methodist Hymnal* and trends in the church are aware that an issue which surfaces time and again is "sexism" or "inclusive language," or to put it another way, "women's images."

Some argue that women do not identify with a faith that seems as paternalistic and male dominated as much of Christianity has been through the years. They are not only concerned about sermons and hymns that suggest that women are excluded as believers (such as "Rise Up, O Men of God" or "God Rest Ye Merry, Gentlemen"). The concern is deeper. If God is Spirit, they ask, must we think of God as male only?

While Scripture reflects the patriarchal culture of the times in which it was written, the argument continues, is it not true that in the Atonement Christ erased gender distinctions, making male and female equal in God's sight? Is it not true that women prophesied in the New Testament and were among early church leaders?

The United Methodist Church today recognizes that women as well as men have been given the gifts for ministry (including the ordained ministry). But more than this, historic Methodism, in its understanding of Scripture, was among the first of the groups which sensed that God's traits include caring, nurturing and affirming—qualities we often identify as feminine.

In our hymns, especially those written by women, we can trace the emergence of this fuller understanding of God that was often neglected through church history. This development is closely linked with Methodism's frontier revival, camp meeting spirituals and gospel music.

In 1853 a little hymnal was published entitled *Miriam's Timbrel: Or Sacred Songs Suited to Revival Occasions; and also For Anti-slavery, Peace, Temperance and Reform Meetings* (Mansfield, Ohio: E. Smith). The book was a project of the Wesleyan Connection, those radical Methodists who had already left the Methodist Episcopal Church because it was not committed strongly enough to revivalism, feminism, temperance, peace and anti-slavery causes.

No one could accuse *Miriam's Timbrel* of sedate or compromised religion. When the book was published, Methodism, or at least a part of Methodism, believed that revivalism coupled with social reform could literally bring Christ's kingdom on earth (postmillennialism).

> *Awake the song of peace—*
> *Let nations join the strain:*
> *The march of blood and pomp of war,*
> *We will not have again!*
> *(Miriam's Timbrel Hymn #84)*

The very title of the hymnal, *Miriam's Timbrel* (named after Moses' sister who danced, sang and helped lead the children of Israel) indicates its conviction that women were on the front lines of revival, conversion and justice.

Other "songsters" (paperbacks of that era associated with camp meetings and revivals) carried the same themes. They spoke of Jesus as a "spouse" (based on the Song of Solomon, describing Jesus from the perspective of the woman, or the church) and lifted up women of the Bible as examples of faith for the church.

> *When Hannah, press'd with grief,*
> *Pour'd forth her soul in prayer,*
> *She quickly found relief*
> *And left her burden there;*
> *Like her, in every trying case,*
> *Let us approach the throne of grace.*[1]

Women played a crucial role in the Methodist revival from the very earliest days. Susanna Wesley (John and Charles' mother) led religious services in the manse when her husband priest was away (to his consternation). Women were leaders in the Methodist societies in Britain and often "exhorted" (what public speaking was called when it was improper to refer to it as "preaching").

Methodist religion was "Spirit-centered" instead of "Word-centered." It was not rational and codified (as Calvinism) or tradition-bound (as Anglicanism) but free and experiential. It was emotional. It recognized that God's Spirit was poured out on both men and women in the New Testament and that women, as well as men, prophesied. New Testament examples of the place of women in the early church helped Methodist women sense that God had freed them to use their gifts for ministry.

Hymnwriting was just one of those gifts. As the Methodist revival spread across England, women in the evangelical wing of the Anglican Church began to write hymns that affected and were affected by Methodist experiential religion. Charlotte Elliott wrote perhaps the greatest of all invitation hymns, "Just As I Am, Without One Plea" (UMH #357), out of the despair of being an invalid. Frances Havergal wrote "Take My Life, and Let It Be Consecrated" (UMH #399). Katherine Hankey wrote "I Love to Tell the Story" (UMH #156).

We are not certain about the influence women had on early camp meeting spirituals. This is folk music, and few authors and composers are known to us. The themes of many of the camp meeting and revival "songsters" (such as *Miriam's Timbrel*), however, give us reason to believe that women's influence was great.

We do know that America's revivalists (along with some groups like the Quakers) were among the first advocates for women. The evangelist Charles Finney encouraged women to speak and pray in public meetings and founded Oberlin College, the first school in America to grant graduate degrees to women. A number of Methodist institutions followed the Oberlin example. Fort Wayne Female College in Indiana (now Taylor University) was established in 1846 to educate women.

The most radical revivalists and women's advocates, however, found it increasingly difficult to stay within the official structures of Methodism. The Seneca Falls meeting of 1848 that launched the women's rights movement was held at a Wesleyan Methodist church. The Wesleyans, who seceded from the Methodist Episcopal Church in 1846, were ordaining women by the 1860s.

The Salvation Army, another offshoot of Methodism, used women preachers from the beginning. Not the least of these was the English woman Catherine Booth, who authored a thirty-two-page pamphlet in the 1850s entitled "Female Ministry."

The holiness churches, most of which also grew out of Methodism, offered women a place of equality. The Church of the Nazarene granted women the right to preach in its 1894 constitution. During that same era another Wesleyan group, the Church of God (Anderson), reported that twenty percent of its clergy were women.

Within the Methodist Churches (North and South), the Evangelical Church and the United Brethren Church, women, while not accepted as clergy, began influencing the thinking and direction of the church through their commitment to Sunday schools, their interest in reform movements and their work on behalf of missions. Women were also increasingly involved in writing and hymnody.

This was particularly true for women associated with the growing, popular Holiness Movement (an emphasis on a deeper spiritual life derived from Wesley's doctrine of perfection—see chapter thirteen). Many of these groups linked together revivalism, holiness and feminism. The best-read holiness devotional writer of the nineteenth century was the Quaker Hannah Whitall Smith, who, in addition to her famous *The Christian's Secret of a Happy Life* (which sold into the millions), also authored a Bible study entitled "God As Our Mother."

Phoebe Palmer, a friend of Smith and a dominant figure in nineteenth-century Methodism, was a lay evangelist associated with city revivals in the late 1850s. Phoebe Palmer exerted her influence through writing (*The Promise of the Father*, a defense of women's right to preach), editing (*Guide to Holiness*, the best-known of the holiness journals), and her famous Tuesday prayer meetings (which apparently functioned much like a modern-day conference). Persons from across the country, including some of the well-known names of Methodism—Bishop A.B. Simpson, Francis Willard, Nathan Bangs—attended her meetings. Phoebe Palmer almost single-handedly (for good or ill) revived and redirected the Holiness Movement in America and Europe. An estimated twenty-five thousand persons were won to Christ through her ministry.

She also wrote hymns, such as the well-known (though never included in an official Methodist hymnal) "Cleansing Wave."

> *Oh, now I see the crimson wave,*
> *the fountain deep and wide;*
> *Jesus, my Lord, mighty to save,*
> *points to his wounded side.*
>
> *Chorus:*
>
> *The cleansing stream I see, I see!*
> *I plunge, and oh, it cleanseth me;*
> *Oh, praise the Lord, it cleanseth me,*
> *It cleanseth me, yes, cleanseth me.*
>
> *I see the new creation rise,*
> *I hear the speaking blood;*
> *it speaks! polluted nature dies—*
> *sinks 'neath the crimson flood.*

Phoebe Palmer used the images and language of the Wesleys ("the speaking blood," "the blood applied"). Her agenda was Christlikeness and holiness, not feminism as such. She was a feminist and an encourager of women because she realized women's special gifts might truly contribute to the great revival of holiness spreading across the nation.

She especially encouraged her own daughter, Phoebe Palmer Knapp. Knapp (whose husband founded the Metropolitan Life Insurance Company) composed the music to "Cleansing Wave" and a number of other hymns. She shared one of her compositions with a friend, Fanny Crosby, and asked Crosby to write words for it. The result is a favorite of United Methodists and other Christians around the world.

> *Blessed assurance, Jesus is mine!*
> *O what a foretaste of glory divine!*
> *(UMH #369)*

Fanny Crosby (1820-1915) epitomizes the key role women were playing in the popular hymnody of Methodism and the larger evangelical world. Crosby herself, though blind, frequently spoke at camp meetings and rescue missions. Though she was not active in the institutional, political and hierarchical matters of the church (such as annual conferences and General Conferences) Crosby was a friend of many "common people" of Methodism—evangelists, pastors and musicians.

With her eight thousand hymns, Crosby perhaps touched more people in Methodism than any bishop, professor, pastor or editor. Despite the reluctance of official Methodism to recognize either women or gospel hymns, five of Crosby's hymns appeared in the 1905 Methodist hymnal, seven in the 1935 hymnal, nine in the 1966 hymnal, and seven in the new hymnal. The 1935 United Brethren hymnal contained thirteen of her hymns and many evangelical hymnals, even today, carry as many as twenty-five of Crosby's hymns.

The influence of persons such as Phoebe Palmer and Fanny Crosby brought a proliferation of female Methodist hymnwriters. Mary D. James, a friend of Phoebe Palmer, wrote "My Body, Mind, and Spirit" and "All For Jesus." Mrs. C.H. Morris, who is in the United Methodist tradition by virtue of being a Methodist Protestant, wrote nine hundred hymns, the best-known of which are "Let Jesus Come into Your Heart," "Stranger of Galilee" and "Sweeter As the Years Go By." Martha Stockton, whose husband John Stockton also wrote hymns ("Come, Every Soul by Sin Oppressed"), wrote "God Loved a World of Sinners Lost." Elvina Hall (1820-1889) wrote the popular "Jesus Paid It All." Priscilla Owens (1829-1907) wrote "We Have Heard the Joyful Sound" and "Will Your Anchor Hold in the Storms of Life?" Louisa Stead (1850-1917) wrote "'Tis So Sweet to Trust in Jesus" (UMH #462).

Mary Lathbury (1841-1913) wrote "Break Thou the Bread of Life" (UMH #599) and "Day Is Dying in the West." The latter hymn was introduced by the famous gospel singer George Stebbins at the Chautauqua Institution in New York, with which Lathbury was associated. Mary Lathbury's reformist thrust is evident in her postmillennial hymn "Arise and Shine":

> *Lift up, lift up thy voice with singing,*
> *dear land, with strength lift up thy voice!*
> *The kingdoms of the earth are bringing*
> *their treasures to thy gates—rejoice!*
> *And shall his flock with strife be riven?*
> *shall envious lines his church divide,*
> *when he, the Lord of earth and heaven,*

> *stands at the door to claim his bride?*
>
> *Chorus:*
>
> *Arise and shine in youth immortal,*
> *thy light is come, thy King appears!*
> *Beyond the century's swinging portal,*
> *breaks a new dawn—the thousand years!*
> *(Ira Sankey's Gospel Hymns No. 1 to 6, #103)*

In fact, a flood of women hymnwriters emerged in the latter half of the nineteenth century, many of whom were Methodist. Official Methodism—the Methodism of colleges, General Conferences and hymnal committees—was very reluctant to endorse their hymns, mostly because they were gospel, associated with the revival and holiness wing of the church, and considered cheap, effeminate and sentimental. At the same time many of these hymns and hymnwriters became mainstays of the evangelical movement and independent evangelical hymnals.

This phenomena can be illustrated by comparing the number of hymns written by women appearing in official and unofficial hymnals. Less than two percent of the hymns in Methodism's 1848 hymnal were written by women. Only seven percent of hymns in the 1878 M.E. hymnal were by women writers. On the other hand, nearly one-third of the songs in the Ira Sankey songbooks were the work of women. In other gospel songbooks, the percentage ranges from twenty-five percent to nearly fifty percent.

The question arises, did these women write different kinds of hymns than their male counterparts? Did they have different emphases or appeal to different biblical images?

Images of Women Hymnwriters

A look at one hundred different hymns by women in Sankey's *Gospel Hymns No. 1 to 6* suggests that, indeed, such differences existed. These differences, combined with other doctrinal shifts of the period (for example, the switch from postmillennialism to premillennialism), were great enough to have a definite effect on how the evangelical world viewed God, sin and salvation. These different emphases make it possible to talk about women's images. (For the word study on these hymns see the table in chapter fourteen.)

What were some of these differences?

1. Women wrote fewer hymns on battles, wars and crusades and more hymns on home, family and children. The word "home" appears forty-four times in the hundred hymns, almost always in reference to heaven. The word "child" or "children" appears twelve times. There are references to "little ones," "loved ones," "lost ones" and "taking the hand." Men also wrote on these themes, but more women than men wrote hymns such as:

> *O child of God, how peacefully*
> *He calms thy fears to rest,*
> *And draws thee upward tenderly,*
> *Where dwell the pure and blest;*
> *And He who bendeth silently*
> *Above the gloom of night,*
> *Will take thee home where endless joy*
> *Shall fill thy soul with light.*
> ("O Child of God," Fanny Crosby)

2. Many more references to an intimate and personal love appeared in the hymns of women.

> *Jesus loves me! this I know,*
> *for the Bible tells me so.*
> (Anna Warner, UMH #191)

Many gospel hymns became love songs to Jesus. They were addressed to Jesus, dedicated to Jesus or used Jesus' love as a theme. "My Jesus, I Love Thee" would be an example.

In the hymns studied which were written by women, sometimes the love imagery went to extremes: Jesus "lulls my troubled soul to rest," I live in the "rapturous heights of his love" and "in his loving embrace." There are, of course, a number of references to "breast" or "bosom." One example from the pen of Fanny Crosby is a hymn which may have been played or sung at more funerals in the last one hundred years than any other hymn:

> *Safe in the arms of Jesus,*
> *safe on His gentle breast,*
> *there by His love o'er-shaded,*
> *sweetly my soul shall rest.*

These are the hymns that gave traditionalists apoplexy. They seemed to sentimentalize and cheapen religion, taking liberties that mortals ought not to take with a holy God. In contrast to this close intimacy and friendship with Jesus is the wholly-other God of some of our worship hymns.

> *Immortal, invisible, God only wise,*
> *in light inaccessible hid from our eyes.*
> *(UMH #103)*

Quite possibly there is room for both kinds of hymns—hymns which stress the awesome, transcendent holiness of God, and hymns which emphasize the close, intimate relationship we can have with him through the shed blood of Jesus Christ. Women writers, particularly, have helped us appreciate the latter.

3. Men and women hymnwriters tended to view sin differently. The Anglicans, Isaac Watts, the Calvinists, the Wesleys—most of Christianity to this point—wasted no effort in pointing out that our sinfulness makes us wretched creatures ("worms" is a favorite word of Watts), actively rebelling against God and quite unworthy of the least of his favors.

However, somewhere in American Methodism (and much of evangelicalism) sinners became not so much miserable wretches as lost wanderers. God was not so much the wrathful judge as the Father awaiting the prodigal. Women hymnwriters helped bring this new insight into our understanding of the nature of sin.

Of the one hundred hymns by women writers researched, no fewer than six use being lost at sea and needing a Savior as the general theme (Mary. A. Baker's "Master, the Tempest Is Raging" is an example). Other biblical stories that are repeated are the prodigal son and the God who stands outside the door and knocks. In Josephine Pollard's hymn "I Stood Outside the Gate," the Savior is in the guise of a "she," who weeps for the sinner, who is seen as a child.

> *I stood outside the gate,*
> *A poor wayfaring child,*
> *Within my heart there beats*
> *A tempest loud and wild.*
> *"Mercy!" I loudly cried;*
> *"Oh, give me rest from sin!"*
> *"I will," a voice replied,*

And Mercy let me in.
She bound my bleeding wounds,
And carried all my sin,
She eased my burdened soul,
Then Jesus took me in.

In Mercy's guise I knew
The Saviour long abused,
Who often sought my heart,
And wept when I refused.
(The Revivalist #488)

At a time when Methodist women were denied entry to the ordained ministry, or a place in the political (the General Conference, for example) and educational structures of the church, they were making important contributions in reform movements, missions and hymn writing. Their efforts helped launch the modern feminist movement. Their use of images such as "home," "family," "children" and "taking the hand," along with their concern for the "lost," whether "lost seamen" or "lost children," and their vision of a nurturing, caring God defined the evangelical movement in nineteenth- and twentieth-century America.

This suggests that more is involved in "women's images" than whether we should address God as "Mother" or rewrite the Bible to conform to feminist ideology. Some people on the fringe, it is true, take the feminist cause to the extreme, recommending that we eliminate words like "Father," "King" and even "Lord" from our everyday Christian language and avoid using any male pronouns for God.

Others are willing to talk about "Father God" if we give equal time to "Mother God." Still others would reinterpret the historic doctrine of the Trinity by baptizing or ordaining in some name other than the biblically mandated "Father, Son and Holy Spirit."

But we do not have to accept extremist views to believe that something about a male-biased, secular society skews our thinking about scriptural truth. The matter of women's images and inclusive language does merit our attention.

The Modernist Reaction

While the issue of women's images today is often associated with various forms of theological liberalism, there is irony in the fact that women's images one hundred years ago were linked with evangelical theology. Much of the inherent sexism of the church's recent past is due not to the evangelical view of faith, but to the liberal revisionism that characterized the first half of the twentieth century.

It has been suggested that official Methodism, the Methodism of conferences, colleges and hymnal committees, became less enthusiastic about revivalism and gospel music as the nineteenth century progressed. With the coming of the twentieth century and the commitment of much of official Methodism to ideologies of modernism (see chapter seven), criticism of Methodism's evangelical past became more and more pronounced.

Part of this criticism focused on hymns and their images. Not only were modernists (and those who followed them) uncomfortable with themes such as "blood," "heaven and hell" and "redemption," but they also raised questions about the very nature of God and Jesus.

I remember reading a book by the famous modernist Harry Emerson Fosdick. The book was *The Manhood of the Master,*[2] and the title accurately describes the contents. True to the theology of the modernists, Fosdick was not interested in the Incarnation, the Atonement nor the second coming of Jesus. He focused on the character and personality of Jesus, and the qualities that followers of Jesus should emulate. For him, these traits were the heart of Christianity. The chapters in the book—Magnanimity, Indignation, Loyalty to His Cause, Power of Endurance, Sincerity, Self-Restraint, Fearlessness—indicate qualities associated with men. Fosdick does not mention qualities that might be associated with women: caring, forgiving, nurturing, loving, giving, self-sacrificing.

Indeed, such qualities, especially as they were suggested by gospel hymns (many of which were written by women), were inadequate for what modernists liked to call the "new age." The "new age" would be ushered in by the birth of a "new man," of which Jesus was the prototype.

> *These things shall be: a loftier race*
> *Than e'er the world hath known shall rise*
> *With flame of freedom in their souls*
> *And light of knowledge in their eyes.*
>
> *They shall be gentle, brave, and strong,*

To spill no drop of blood, but dare
All that may plant man's lordship firm
On earth and fire and sea and air.
(The Book of Hymns #198)

A good definition for this "new age" ideology might be "Hairy Chest Theology." It posited a "super race" in which "men" would be self-sufficient, strong, intelligent and cultured. The favorite words in the hymns of this era (see chapter fourteen) were brave, true, strong, loyal and noble. There was little need to talk about being "safe in the arms of Jesus," or for "amazing grace that saved a wretch like me." This was a roll-up-the-sleeves and gird-up-the-loins and bring-in-the-kingdom sort of religion. This was "Rise up, O men of God! Have done with lesser things," and "'Are ye able,' said the Master, 'to be crucified with me?'"

God send us men whose aim 'twill be
Not to defend some ancient creed,
But to live out the laws of Christ
In every thought and word and deed.
(The Book of Hymns #191)

Jesus, in this ideology, was not "Blessed Redeemer" or "Lover of my soul," but "young and fearless prophet," "Master of the waking world" or "Master workman of the race." The key phrase, repeated over and over, was "Fatherhood of God and Brotherhood of Man." This implied universalism had little need to talk about the church because "brotherhood" referred not just to believers but to everybody.

For what are sundering strains of blood,
Or ancient caste and creed?
One claim unites all men in God
To serve each human need.

To this clear call of brotherhood
Our hearts responsive ring;
We join the glorious new crusade
Of our great Lord and King.
(The Book of Hymns #189)

Obviously this ideology had little love for either gospel hymns or the insights of the women authors who wrote them. Gospel hymns, in this way of thinking, were concerned with personal salvation instead of social salvation; they spoke of Jesus dying on the cross as a substitute for sin, rather than as an heroic example of goodness and dedication to a cause. Very few women wrote hymns for the social gospel movement.

Modernism and the social gospel made some valid contributions to the life of the church, such as the concern for social justice and the need to be relevant to the times. Its easy optimism, however, unraveled under the horrors of World War II in the same way that Methodist postmillennialism unraveled under the horrors of the Civil War. It stands today as a failed theology. It bequeathed to the church several popular hymns ("God of Grace and God of Glory," for example) but its predominantly male images were among the first to give way to feminist criticism.

To Do

Perhaps the best way to study the new effort to include women's images in hymns is to examine several of the new, contemporary hymns in the hymnal. These include the following:

"Wellspring of Wisdom" (UMH #506)

"Woman in the Night" (UMH #274)

"O God Who Shaped Creation" (UMH #443)

"To a Maid Engaged to Joseph" (UMH #215)

"Canta, Debora, Canta" (UMH #81)

"The Care the Eagle Gives Her Young" (UMH #118)

"How Like a Gentle Spirit" (UMH #115)

"Source and Sovereign, Rock and Cloud" (UMH #113)

Do these hymns capture biblical truths and insights that have been missing in previous hymns?

Eleven

Christian Essentials

At church camp, I was beginning a study of United Methodist beliefs. I asked the teenagers to write down what they understood to be the most important doctrines or teachings of the church.

Groans ensued: "This is just like school." But dutifully, if not enthusiastically, they began expounding their high school version of United Methodism: God (we believe in him), prayer (we're for it), baptizing babies and dancing if we don't overdo it.

But Beverly, despite being a long-time United Methodist and popular district UMYF officer, was stumped. I tried to encourage her by mental telepathy: Try to remember the pastors' sermons, Sunday school lessons or confirmation class. She was still stumped. Finally, her face lit up and she wrote two words. I was curious about what two words would sum up over two hundred years of Methodist history.

Her answer? "Total Abstinence."

There is certainly nothing wrong with total abstinence. I, for one, am for it. But there is surely more to United Methodist doctrine than total abstinence.

Roman Catholics, when asked about their faith, remember teachings from catechism. Lutherans refer to the creeds. Baptists can usually think of a verse or two of Scripture. But United Methodists too often do little more than offer vague opinions.

There are reasons for this. The Methodist movement did not spring from doctrinal controversy. John Wesley had no argument with the historic faith of the Church of England as that faith was summarized in the Articles of Religion. Methodism was a revival movement through which the Holy Spirit made personal in hearts the truths which many at that time confessed only formally and intellectually. When asked to describe a Methodist, Wesley would talk about how a person lived and his or her experience with Christ. Concerning doctrine, Wesley's comment was, "But as to all opinions that do not strike at the root of Christianity, we think and let think."

That statement has sometimes been interpreted to mean Methodists do not emphasize doctrine because one belief is as good as another. That interpretation is misleading. John Wesley, though broad-minded in many ways, confessed historic and traditional Christianity and expected his followers to do the same. When he mentioned "opinions that do not strike at the root of Christianity," he was assuming there is a root, an essential core of doctrine, that distinguishes Christianity from other religions. That essential core is the teaching of the apostles as interpreted by the early church and ecumenical councils and found in creeds such as the Apostles' Creed and Nicene Creed. It was transmitted through reformers such as Martin Luther and John Calvin and summarized in statements such as the Thirty-nine Articles of the Church of England (the basis for the Articles of Religion of the Methodist Church).

That essential core is basically a story, the story of God's self-revelation through what might be called the great events of salvation history. It is the story of Creation, the Fall, the Call of Abraham, the Exodus, the Covenant at Sinai and other Old Testament events that lead up to the birth, death and resurrection of Jesus Christ, Pentecost and the birth of the church. Doctrines, or teachings, are interpretations of that story that help us understand who God is, who we are and how we can be reconciled to God.

At least three levels of doctrines or teachings should be considered:

1. Doctrines or teachings which are basic to Christian faith. John Wesley referred to these as "essentials," or the "core of doctrine." United Methodists share these beliefs with all Christians, whether Roman Catholic or Nazarene or Baptist. They are the doctrinal basis of our oneness in Christ. Examples would be the doctrines of the Trinity and the Incarnation.

2. Doctrines or teachings which are either unique to Methodists historically or which grew out of the Methodist experience in such a way that they are identified as United Methodist distinctives. An example would be the Methodist doctrines of holiness and assurance.

3. Doctrines or teachings which have been emphasized by different groups within the church but on which not all United Methodists agree. The diversity of United Methodism is clearly seen in these teachings. They are the "non-essentials" about which there may be a number of opinions. Interpretations of the details of the second coming of Christ or the meaning of peace with justice are examples.

How do we learn the truths or teachings of Christian faith? We learn themthrough stories told in Sunday school, sermons and discussion groups, books and formal study, table talk in Christian homes, the example set by the way Christians live and conversations—formal and informal—with other Christians.

We also learn Christian truth through hymns. For United Methodists who have no official catechism the hymnal becomes a catechism. Since United Methodists are not known for formal statements of faith, the hymns function as a statement of faith. Hymns are prayers, testimonies, sermons and summaries of scriptural truth we hold dear. The Wesleys wrote hymns and encouraged their use whenever Methodist people gathered largely to teach the faith. In the preface of the 1790 hymnal, John Wesley wrote,

> In what other publication of the kind, have you so distinct and full account of Scriptural Christianity? Such declarations of the heights and depths of Religion, speculative and practical? So strong cautions against the most plausible errors, particularly those that are now most prevalent? And so clear directions for making sure your calling and election sure; for perfecting holiness in the fear of God?

For this reason, then, we study hymns to understand the faith we profess.

Essential Beliefs

The United Methodist General Conference of 1988 adopted a new doctrinal statement which clarified the doctrinal standards of

United Methodism. These standards can be found in the *Discipline*, paragraph 68. They include the Articles of Religion of the Methodist Church, the Confession of Faith of the Evangelical United Brethren Church and Wesley's *Sermons* and *Notes on the New Testament*. From these doctrinal standards and the writings of John Wesley, we are able to discuss the United Methodist understanding of "essential beliefs."

What are those beliefs? They are several, and their importance is evident in the hymns we sing. *The United Methodist Hymnal* is a particularly rich resource.

Incarnation: The Deity of Christ

The heart of the gospel proclaims that the eternal God became incarnate in the person of Jesus of Nazareth. We most often sing about the mysteries and wonder of the Incarnation at Christmastime.

> *Christ, by highest heaven adored;*
> *Christ, the everlasting Lord,*
> *late in time behold him come,*
> *offspring of the virgin's womb.*
> *Veiled in flesh the Godhead see,*
> *hail th' incarnate Deity,*
> *pleased with us in flesh to dwell,*
> *Jesus, our Emmanuel.*
> *(UMH #240)*

The poetry of this beloved carol reminds us of the Apostles' Creed: ". . . conceived by the Holy Spirit, born of the Virgin Mary."

Many hymns we sing at Christmas concern not only who Jesus is, but why he came.

> *Born thy people to deliver,*
> *born a child and yet a King,*
> *born to reign in us forever,*
> *now thy gracious kingdom bring.*
> *By thine own eternal spirit*
> *rule in all our hearts alone;*
> *by thine all-sufficient merit,*
> *raise us to thy glorious throne.*
> *(UMH #196)*

Other hymns describe events before the Christmas story and

reflect on the pre-existence of Christ. "Of the Father's Love Begotten," from the fifth century, echoes ideas in the Nicene Creed.

> *Of the Father's love begotten,*
> *e're the worlds began to be,*
> *he is Alpha and Omega,*
> *he the source, the ending he;*
> *of the things that are, that have been,*
> *and that future years shall see,*
> *evermore and evermore.*
> *(UMH #184)*

Christmas is a special season for United Methodists, and for all Christians, because the event it celebrates, the birth of Jesus Christ, points to his deity and the truth of the Incarnation.

Original Sin: The Fallenness of Humankind

If we associate Christmas and the birth of Christ with joyous celebration, we associate Good Friday and the story of Christ's death on the cross with lament and shame. This is because we realize that our own rebellion and sin made the crucifixion necessary.

> *Died he for me, who caused his pain?*
> *For me, who him to death pursued?*
> *(UMH #363)*

The Bible teaches that because of the sin of our first parents (the Fall), all have subsequently sinned and fall short of the glory of God (Romans 3:23). The doctrine of Original Sin is not an article of faith to be confessed in a creed as much as it is a recognition that, despite our best efforts, we are separated from God. We live in a fallen world, and we cannot save ourselves from the consequences of sin.

Earlier Methodist hymnals expressed this doctrine powerfully and without compromise.

> *Lord, we are vile, conceived in sin,*
> *and born unholy and unclean;*
> *sprung from the man whose guilty fall*
> *corrupts his race and taints us all.*
>
> *Soon as we draw our infant breath*

the seeds of sin grow up for death;
thy law demands a perfect heart,
but we're defiled in every part.
("Lord, We Are Vile" by Charles Wesley, in Methodist
   hymnals until 1905)

"Lord, We Are Vile" is from the section in earliest Methodist
hymnals headed "Depravity." In the 1849 hymnal, this section had
eighteen hymns; 123 hymns were classified as "The Sinner," with
subheadings for "Depravity," "Awakening," "Inviting" and
"Penitential."
Our preaching and singing may be less condemning of human
nature today, but our hymns, when read carefully, still confess to
our lostness apart from the grace of Jesus Christ.

Just as I am, poor, wretched, blind;
sight, riches, healing of the mind,
yea, all I need, in thee to find.
O Lamb of God, I come, I come!
(UMH #357)

The great mystery, repeated so often in our hymns, is how
fallen humankind can have an opportunity to be children of God.

O how shall I the goodness tell,
Father, which thou to me hast showed?
That I, a child of wrath and hell,
I should·be called a child of God!
(UMH #342)

Curiously, there is an effort today to downplay the doctrine of
Original Sin. Some people argue that talk about Original Sin
creates unnecessary feelings of guilt and inadequacy in people.
But Christians emphasize that while we acknowledge ourselves
as sinners, we also are loved by God. We are so precious in his
sight that, in the person of Jesus Christ, he sacrificed his life for
us.
The doctrine of Original Sin is not an argument that the created
world is without a great deal of goodness and nobility. Rather, it
contends that even when we are at our best, we are spiritually lost
without the grace of God. This Wesley hymn says it well:

Sinners, turn: why will you die?

God, the Spirit, asks you why; . . . .
You, on whom he favors showers,
you, possessed of nobler powers,
you, of reason's powers possessed,
you, with will and memory blest,
you, with finer sense endued,
creatures capable of God;
noblest of his creatures, why,
why will you forever die?
(UMH #346)

Even our most valiant efforts cannot atone for sin.

Not the labors of my hands
can fulfill thy law's demands;
could my zeal no respite know,
could my tears forever flow,
all for sin could not atone;
thou must save, and thou alone.
(UMH #361)

The Atonement: Christ Died for Our Sins

Fortunately, a discussion of sin leads to God's remedy for sin—the cross.

Perhaps no other doctrine is as crucial to the Christian faith as the truth that Christ died for our sins. The Atonement is, unfortunately, played down in much of modern theology. When the church's preaching and proclamation primarily emphasize politics, social action or self-actualization, the doctrine of Christ's death for sin suffers. We must remind ourselves from time to time that there is no salvation without the cross, no forgiveness of sin without atonement and no Christianity without Christ's death. This is what the apostle Paul had in mind in 1 Corinthians 15:3: "For what I received I passed on to you as of first importance: that Christ died for our sins according to the Scriptures." The "gospel," or "good news," that Christians so often talk about is the good news that God has acted to erase the sins of the world in the cross of Jesus Christ.

Because of this, the cross is the symbol of the Christian faith. We put crosses on our altars, our steeples and jewelry around our necks to indicate this one essential truth that stands above all. Whatever else we affirm, first and foremost we affirm the cross.

Paul writes, "For I resolved to know nothing while I was with you except Jesus Christ and him crucified" (1 Corinthians 2:2). If there is an incarnation, it happened so there can be atonement.

Is it any wonder, then, that our hymns and their titles are full of references to the cross?

"The Old Rugged Cross"
"When I Survey the Wondrous Cross"
"Cross of Jesus, Cross of Sorrow"
"In the Cross of Christ I Glory"
"Jesus, Keep Me Near the Cross"

The Incarnation and the Atonement (the cross) divide the Bible into Old and New Testaments (or Old and New Covenants). The Incarnation and the Atonement divide time into B.C. and A.D., before Christ and after Christ. In contrast to religions which teach salvation through some form of self-effort or trying harder, Christians teach that salvation is an act of God accomplished through the cross and made available to us by grace through faith.

How does this happen? The mystery is so great it defies rational explanation, but its essence is suggested in what are sometimes called the three major theories or teachings about the Atonement. The three complement each other and are intertwined in Scripture and in our hymns.

Christ As Example: Moral Influence

The Moral Influence theory of the Atonement is often associated with theological liberalism. Whatever else we may say about Jesus of Nazareth, we start with the truth that his life gives us an example of how to live.

> *O young and fearless Prophet of ancient Galilee:*
> *thy life is still a summons to serve humanity.*
> *(UMH #444)*

We are called to live and sacrifice even as Christ did.

> *"Are ye able," said the Master,*
> *"to be crucified with me?"*
> *"Yea," the sturdy dreamers answered,*
> *"to the death we follow thee."*
> *(UMH #530)*

Christ As Victor: Ransom

Our teaching about the meaning of the life, death and resurrection of Jesus Christ recognizes the cosmic spiritual struggle between God and Satan, or between good and evil. The cross and resurrection of Christ is the ransom cost, the sacrifice given to break Satan's power and redeem humankind and all of earth.

> *This child, now weak in infancy,*
> *our confidence and joy shall be,*
> *the power of Satan breaking,*
> *our peace eternal making.*
> *(UMH #223)*

Hymns and Scripture often use images of warfare to point to this truth.

> *The strife is o'er, the battle done;*
> *the victory of life is won;*
> *the song of triumph has begun.*
> *Alleluia!*
> *The powers of death have done their worst,*
> *But Christ their legions hath dispersed;*
> *let shouts of holy joy outburst:*
> *Alleluia! (UMH #306)*

At the same time, mysteriously and paradoxically, God's weapon of warfare is the oposite of what the world might expect: The blood of Jesus brings life out of death, strength out of weakness, victory out of defeat.

Jesus As the Lamb Sacrificed: Substitution

The teaching of the cross most identified with evangelical preaching and teaching, ad to which the overwhelming majority of our hymns refer, is that of Jesus as the Lamb of God who suffers the penalty and consequences of sin in our place so that we might be forgiven. Christ fulfills the Old Testament demand for sacrifice to turn aside the wrath of God and make possible our forgiveness.

> *O Love divine, what hast thou done!*
> *Th'immortal God hath died for me!*
> *The Father's coeternal Son*
> *bore all my sins upon the tree.*
> *Th'immortal God for me hath died:*
> *my Lord, my Love, is crucified!*
> *(UMH #287)*

Basic to this teaching on the Atonement is a moral sense that when something goes wrong in the world, someone is responsible, or guilty, and ought to pay for the wrong. If a crime is committed, the guilty party should make it right (make atonement) or at least suffer consequences for the wrong done. Murderers should be brought to trial and sinners should be brought to judgment.

The Bible teaches that God, through Jesus Christ, took all the world's hurt and wrong and sin upon himself. He paid the price, so that the wrath and death and hell due us might be put aside and we may be reconciled to him.

> *And when I think that God, his Son not sparing,*
> *sent him to die, I scarce can take it in,*
> *that on the cross, my burden gladly bearing,*
> *he bled and died to take away my sin.*
> *(UMH #77)*

The cost of forgiveness falls on the person who does the forgiving. For example, if a man runs a stop sign and wrecks my car, justice demands that he pay, either out of his own pocket or through his insurance company. But if he has no insurance and I forgive him, it is I who pay to repair my car. Under justice we would receive due penalty for our sins—death and hell—but under forgiveness, the cost of the crime is paid by the forgiver, in this case, God through Jesus Christ.

> *Was it for crimes that I have done,*
> *he groaned upon the tree?*
> *Amazing pity! grace unknown!*
> *And love beyond degree!*
> *(UMH #359)*

To Do

1. One argument for using *The United Methodist Hymnal* is that it, unlike many independently published hymn books, makes an effort to cover the great events of the church year and the doctrines that go with them. So, for example, there are a large number of Christmas hymns that teach the doctrine of the Incarnation. Almost none of these hymns are "gospel hymns." They come from a different milieu, a "catholic" or high church tradition. Many of the writers are from the Church of England. Why is this?

2. Our hymnal, while it often refers to the fact that we are born in sin and need salvation, has omitted a section on depravity that appeared in earlier Methodist hymnals. Why is this? Does the removal of such sections help or hinder the faith?

3. The following hymns or hymn verses discuss the cross. Which theory of the Atonement does each reflect?

"What Wondrous Love Is This" (UMH #292, v. 1)

"Behold the Savior of Mankind" (UMH #293)

"Beneath the Cross of Jesus" (UMH #297, v. 2)

"Ah, Holy Jesus" (UMH #289)

"O Sacred Head, Now Wounded" (UMH #286)

"Sing, My Tongue, the Glorious Battle" (UMH #296, v. 1)

"'Tis Finished! The Messiah Dies" (UMH #282)

"Were You There?" (UMH #288)

4. How do the doctrines of Incarnation, Original Sin and the Atonement fare in your church's preaching and teaching? Are these truths clearly taught and understood?

Twelve

More Christian Essentials

"You don't have to believe anything to be a United Methodist." It was an offhand remark, spoken in a ministerial meeting. It drew a few chuckles, and that made it even worse. A Christian Church minister, a Lutheran, a Roman Catholic and several others—all gave approval to the characterization with their smiles.

When I heard a similar statement made in a United Methodist gathering, it drew a facetious rejoinder: "Not true. We do believe in something. We believe you have to pay apportionments and order the denominational Sunday school material."

But United Methodists were not always known as doctrinal lightweights. The doctrinal beliefs of early Methodist preachers were carefully examined. Conferences frequently reported that pastors (and laypersons) were removed from their duties because their preaching and teaching was not consistent with the doctrinal standards of the church. Only in recent decades has "doctrine"— the essence of what is taught and preached—been depreciated.

There are several reasons for this:

1. Many in the church have feared that an overemphasis on doctrine could lead to cold formalism and rationalism. Methodism has always been known as a movement with a "vital" faith. It was more a religion of the heart than the head. In contrast, other movements, Lutheranism and Calvinism, had their periods of "scholasticism" in which head knowledge became more important

than heart knowledge. Some have argued that Methodism should never be guilty of that.

2. Methodism throughout the nineteenth century became increasingly committed to moral and ethical concerns, everything from the use of alcohol to the problems of unemployment. Many thought that an undue emphasis on doctrine would detract from Methodism's social and ethical witness.

3. In the early part of the twentieth century, the fundamentalist-modernist controversy split several denominations. At the heart of the controversy was disagreement over what were the irreducible truths of the faith. Many sought to protect the unity of the church by discouraging discussion of potentially divisive doctrinal issues.

4. With the coming of the twentieth century a portion of Methodism caught up in various forms of liberalism became convinced that the historic faith was no longer relevant. These Methodists had difficulty getting excited about doctrines about which they had severe doubts. As one Methodist asserted, "Doctrinal statements should be shrouded in ambiguity so that we can interpret their meaning however seems best to us."

Perhaps the low point in the history of Methodism's doctrine came with the 1972 doctrinal statement, which served the church until a new and more traditional statement was adopted in 1988. The 1972 statement grew out of the merger of the Methodist and Evangelical United Brethren denominations and was intended to give the newly merged church a focus for "a new day."

Unfortunately, the statement did more blurring than focusing. It was adopted by the 1972 General Conference by a vote of 923 to 17, without debate or attempted amendment. This rushed manner suggested that the church thought it had many more important things to concern itself with than the specifics of the faith it confessed. The statement substituted process for content (how we go about determining what we believe is more important than what we believe), depreciated the role of "doctrinal standards," introduced the idea that anything goes (pluralism), and spoke of the "core of doctrine" or the "essentials of the faith" without defining what those essentials are. The result was doctrinal confusion in a fragmented and declining church.

During this time, and indeed throughout the history of United Methodism, the hymnal served as a stabilizing force for faith, especially as it provided congregations with a point of contact with the historic and essential truths of Christianity. The church sang what it found difficult to confess in formal statements. Regardless of the ambiguity that often emanated from teaching materials and pulpits, the hymns testified to a rich doctrinal heritage and helped Methodists identify with the mainstream of ecumenical faith.

This chapter looks at three more of what John and Charles Wesley and early Methodists understood to be "essentials" of the faith. These teachings are not uniquely United Methodist, but they are truths shared by all Christian groups, whether denominations or para-church ministries, whether North American or Asian or African, whether in the twentieth century, the fifth century or the twenty-third century.

The New Birth

Father Skip of St. Vincent's Roman Catholic Church had participated in our United Methodist Sunday morning service. It was the early 1970s, and contacts with Roman Catholics were still fairly new for most of us Protestants. But the experience had been good. We had shared a dialogue about the truths that both United Methodists and Roman Catholics confess.

When the service was over, Father Skip suddenly said, "Don't take off your robe. I want you now to come to St. Vincent's and preach for me."

"Preach?" It was 10:45, and I knew his service started at 11:00. I must have sounded surprised, because my going to his church had never been discussed. "What do you want me to preach about?"

"Preach on what United Methodists have to offer Roman Catholics in this new day of Christian understanding."

What an assignment! I felt a sense of panic. There would be a thousand people at the 11:00 Mass, and I had nothing prepared. My file of old sermons did not include any messages outlining what United Methodists had to offer Roman Catholics.

Then the inspiration came. Of course. The new birth. I could tell the story of John Wesley, Aldersgate and the heart strangely warmed. The changed life! That is not a "Methodist" teaching really. It is a Christian teaching. We can be born again. Not only can we be born again, according to John 3:7 we *must* be born again. That simple message is a legitimate United Methodist contribution to the larger Christian community.

Among the themes preached by John and Charles Wesley and other early Methodists, none was addressed as frequently as that of the new birth. One is tempted to call this a Methodist distinctive emphasis, since the Methodists emphasized the new birth more than any other group.

For Wesley, however, the new birth was not a Methodist peculiarity, it was a Christian truth meant for believers everywhere. Behind John Wesley's oft-quoted statement, "If your heart is as my heart, give me your hand," is the understanding that it is the new birth that is a major basis of unity. Opinions divide, non-essential beliefs divide, but the experience of Christ in the heart, whether Lutheran or Roman Catholic or Methodist, unites.

This important truth so possessed early Methodists that they produced a virtual explosion of hymns, spirituals and choruses centered on the theme of the new birth.

> *On this glad day the glorious Sun*
> *of Righteousness arose,*
> *on my benighted soul he shone*
> *and filled it with repose.*
> *(UMH #58)*

> *'Tis Love! 'tis Love! thou diedst for me.*
> *I hear thy whisper in my heart.*
> *The morning breaks, the shadows flee,*
> *pure, Universal Love thou art.*
> *(UMH #386)*

It can be argued that Wesley's major poems, such as "O For a Thousand Tongues to Sing" (see chapter three), and "Come, O Thou Traveler Unknown" are treatises on the new birth. But this was true for hymns other than Wesley music. Many of our best-loved hymns celebrate the new birth. Some are old.

> *Amazing grace! How sweet the sound*
> *that saved a wretch like me!*
> *I once was lost, but now am found;*
> *was blind, but now I see.*
> *(UMH #378)*

Some are more recent.

> *He touched me, O he touched me,*

> *and O the joy that floods my soul;*
> *something happened, and now I know,*
> *he touched me and made me whole.*
> *(UMH #367)*

Nineteenth-century Methodism's preoccupation with preaching, teaching and singing on the new birth eventually caused a backlash. Critics claimed that these hymns were experience-centered and individualistic to the extent that other aspects of the gospel were overlooked.

There is truth to the charge. Any discussion of the new birth must emphasize that it is more than a crisis conversion experience. Christian nurture, ongoing worship, the sacraments and fruits of the changed life are also necessary ingredients of what we call the new birth.

The means of God's life-giving grace (the new birth) are celebrated in hymns on the sacraments.

> *We your people stand before you,*
> *water-washed and Spirit-born.*
> *By your grace, our lives we offer.*
> *Recreate us; God, transform!*
> *(UMH #605)*

A number of other well-known hymns give witness to "new life." These are also quite properly a part of the doctrine of the new birth.

> *Breathe on me, Breath of God,*
> *fill me with life anew;*
> *that I may love what thou dost love,*
> *and do what thou wouldst do.*
> *(UMH #420)*

Finally, Methodists historically have argued that if God can transform an individual he can also transform society. Opinions may differ as to how this comes about, but ultimately we pray with the Methodist theologian Georgia Harkness:

> *This is my prayer, O Lord of all earth's kingdoms:*
> *thy kingdom come; on earth thy will be done.*
> *Let Christ be lifted up till all shall serve him,*
> *and hearts united learn to live as one.*

O hear my prayer, thou God of all the nations;
myself I give thee; let thy will be done.
(UMH #437)

The Resurrection and Eternal Life

Teaching about the new birth should not be discussed apart from the gracious action of God that makes it possible. That gracious action includes prevenient grace (which prepares us), justifying grace (which declares us righteous before God) and sanctifying grace (God's action to make us holy).

This grace is made possible through the life, death and resurrection of Jesus Christ. Hence the importance of the Christmas, Good Friday and Easter events.

The Easter event is, of course, the Resurrection.

With Christ's resurrection we also teach the possibility of our own new life (new birth) and hope of our own resurrection and eternal life. This is the apostle's point in 1 Corinthians 15:21-22: "For since death came through a man, the resurrection of the dead comes also through a man. For as in Adam all die, so in Christ all will be made alive."

One of the new hymns in the hymnal, from the Spanish tradition, paraphrases the Corinthian verse:

If the Lord had never risen,
we'd have nothing to believe;
but his promise can be trusted:
"You will live, because I live."
As we share the death of Adam,
so in Christ we live again;
death has lost its sting and terror,
Christ the Lord has come to reign.
(UMH #313)

A verse that links together the new birth, the Resurrection and baptism is from the hymn, "We Know That Christ Is Raised" (UMH #610).

We share by water in his saving death.
Reborn, we share with him an Easter life.
Baptized, we live with God the Three in One. Alleluia.

We do not need to be clever and deeply theological in expressing our Easter faith. Christian faith, after all, is basically the telling of God's story, the most important chapter of which is the account of Jesus' death and resurrection. A hymn new to *The United Methodist Hymnal*, which has a chorus-like tune, is the spiritual "They Crucified My Savior" (UMH #316).

They crucified my Savior and nailed him to the tree. . . .

Refrain:

He rose, he rose,
he rose from the dead.
He rose, he rose,
he arose from the dead!
He rose, he rose,
he rose from the dead,
and the Lord will bear my spirit home.

Then Joseph begged his body and laid it in the tomb. . . .

Sister Mary she came running, a-looking for my Lord. . . .

An angel came from heaven and rolled the stone away. . . .

While the resurrection of Christ is a simple story, it is also an event with cosmic and eternal significance. With this in mind, a number of hymns seek to reveal the significance behind the story. Evangelicals might notice that most of these hymns are not of the gospel variety. They tend to be hymns from the catholic tradition. The following hymn by John of Damascus, written about 750 A.D., witnesses to the cosmic implications of the Resurrection ("earth, tell it out abroad."), as well as to the fulfillment of an Old Testament event ("passover"):

The day of resurrection!
Earth, tell it out abroad;
the passover of gladness,
the passover of God.
From death to life eternal,
from earth unto the sky,
our Christ hath brought us over,
with hymns of victory.
(UMH #303)

Christians assert that Christ's resurrection was not just a

"spirit" resurrection—a mere continuing of Jesus' influence and goodness—but a bodily resurrection, an actual coming to life of that which was dead. With this in mind we sing the gospel song:

Up from the grave he arose,
with a mighty triumph o' er his foes.
(UMH #322)

A Charles Wesley hymn placed back in the hymnal also affirms the truth of the Resurrection by describing the Ascension (a part of the Resurrection story that evangelicals often overlook):

Hail the day that sees him rise, Alleluia!
To his throne above the skies, Alleluia!
Christ, awhile to mortals given, Alleluia!
Reascends his native heaven, Alleluia!
(UMH #312)

A discussion of heaven and eternal life also belong properly to the doctrine of the Resurrection, even though in hymnody they are often separated.

Unfortunately, we preach and teach about heaven and eternal life less often than the early Methodists. The 1972 doctrinal statement, for example, made almost no mention of the hope that is ours in the life to come.

Not so in early Methodism. In the Wesleys' music, in camp meeting spirituals (particularly Negro spirituals) and in gospel music, people sang unabashedly about death and heaven. Almost every gospel song or spiritual had a "heaven" verse, with images of coming chariots, crossing the Jordan, new robes, glory land, Canaan and going home.

Oh, fix me,
oh, fix me,
oh, fix me;
fix me, Jesus, fix me.

Fix me for my long white robe,
fix me, Jesus, fix me,
fix me for my starry crown,
fix me, Jesus, fix me.

Fix me for my journey home,
fix me, Jesus, fix me.

> *Fix me for my dying bed,*
> *fix me, Jesus, fix me.*
> *(UMH #655)*

and,

> *When we all get to heaven,*
> *what a day of rejoicing that will be!*
> *When we all see Jesus,*
> *we'll sing and shout the victory.*
> *(UMH #701)*

Because of Christ's resurrection, believers have hope. We do not perish with a world that is transient and passing. We are not only saved from the doubts and fears of this life, but from the consequences of sin—death and hell—to eternal life with Christ who won the victory for us.

The Trinity

The Trinity is sometimes the first doctrine mentioned in a discussion of Christian truth. However, perhaps it is better explained after studying the life of Christ and the entire Christian experience.

The doctrine of the Trinity grew out of reflection by the early church. The God who came in the Spirit at Pentecost is the same God who was seen in Jesus Christ and who revealed himself through the events of the Old Testament.

Thus Christianity's unique understanding of God, which differentiates it from all other religions, is that God has revealed himself in three persons: God the Father of our Lord Jesus Christ who in the Apostles' Creed is described as "maker of heaven and earth"; Jesus Christ, the son of the Father, whom we call "Lord"; and the Holy Spirit.

This understanding of God has been the Christian confession at all times and places. It refutes any form of "Unitarianism," which sees God only as Spirit, or only as the Creator. The Trinitarian confession is the doctrinal basis for Christian cooperation in the World Council of Churches and other ecumenical organizations.

By singing (or saying) the name of the triune God (Father, Son and Holy Spirit) we identify our faith, i.e., Christianity. A Christian wedding ceremony, for example, is conducted in the name of the

Father and of the Son and of the Holy Spirit. The same is true of a Christian baptism, ordination or other Christian service.

Christian worship is not just directed to "God," since a number of religions and ideologies can talk about "God." Our worship is addressed not to just any God, not even to a "God of many names," but to a specific God, a named God, known in his mystery as Father, Son and Holy Spirit. A chorale says it this way:

> *Holy Father, Holy Son,*
> *Holy Spirit: three we name thee,*
> *though in essence only One,*
> *undivided God we claim thee,*
> *and adoring bend the knee,*
> *while we own the mystery.*
> *(UMH #79)*

Unfortunately in much of our worship (particularly in evangelical churches) the naming and celebrating of the triune God is often overlooked. If it is true that the doctrine of the Trinity is so important to Christian faith, shouldn't some form of the Gloria Patri or Doxology be a part of every worship service?

> *Glory be to the Father,*
> *and to the Son,*
> *and to the Holy Ghost;*
> *as it was in the beginning,*
> *is now, and ever shall be,*
> *world without end. Amen. Amen.*
> *(The Gloria Patri)*

and,

> *Praise God from whom all blessings flow,*
> *Praise him, all creatures here below.*
> *Praise him above, ye heavenly host;*
> *Praise Father, Son and Holy Ghost.*
> *(The Doxology)*

Evangelicals, who sometimes tend to subsist on a diet of gospel songs and choruses, need to remember that hymns from the historic churches—Catholic, Lutheran, Orthodox, Anglican—and not hymns from the revival tradition are most faithful to confess the triune God. Evangelicals should realize that we do not sing these hymns for our own encouragement, but rather to glorify and give honor to the triune God.

> *We believe in one true God,*
> *Father, Son, and Holy Ghost,*
> *ever present help in need,*
> *praised by all the heavenly host. . . .*
> *(UMH #85)*

In recent years, out of a feminist concern for "new images" of God and a reaction against masculine words like "Father" and "Son," there has been some experimentation with different kinds of language to speak of the Trinity.

Some of these efforts can be seen in several hymns in *The United Methodist Hymnal* that are new to Methodism. A new version of the Doxology speaks of "God," "Jesus Christ" and the "Spirit" (UMH #94). A hymn, "Source and Sovereign, Rock and Cloud" (UMH #113), uses symbolic representations for each person of the Trinity. Still another, by Episcopal priest Carl Daw Jr., in a somewhat similar way suggests a number of metaphors in verses that begin "God the Spirit," "Christ our Savior" and "Great Creator" (UMH #648).

The key question asked about these hymns (and others) is whether the metaphors complement and enhance "The Name" by glorifying the triune God, or whether the metaphors are meant as name substitutes. An example of the former is the Wesley hymn "Maker, in Whom We Live" (UMH #88), in which the triune God is addressed as "Maker," "Incarnate Deity" and "Spirit of Holiness." An example of the latter would be to baptize, ordain or otherwise offer what is meant to be the Christian signature with a name substitute such as "Creator, Redeemer and Sustainer." Using a false name amounts to practicing a false religion.

The United Methodist Hymnal is fairly cautious at this point, thus placing itself in the mainstream of Christian teaching.

To Do

Christian teaching encompasses many more areas than those mentioned in these chapters on "essentials." These teachings concern the nature and mission of the church, the sacraments, the return of the Lord and other topics. Keeping in mind that hymns are poetic expressions of our faith and are not always meant to be interpreted literally, what conclusions do you draw about the teachings below from reading the hymns that follow?

A. *The Return of the Lord*

"Soon and Very Soon" (UMH # 706)

"My Lord, What a Morning" (UMH #719)

"Lo, He Comes With Clouds Descending" (UMH #718)

"Wake, Awake, for Night Is Flying" (UMH #720)

B. *The Nature of the Church*

"See How Great a Flame Aspires" (UMH #541)

"I Love Thy Kingdom, Lord" (UMH #540)

"In Christ There Is No East or West" (UMH #548)

"O Church of God, United" (UMH #547)

"The Church's One Foundation" (UMH #545)

C. *The Scriptures*

"O Word of God Incarnate" (UMH #598)

"Whether the Word Be Preached or Read" (UMH #595)

"Come, Holy Ghost, Our Hearts Inspire" (UMH #603)

Thirteen

United Methodist Distinctives

I found a treasure in a used book store: an early American edition of the hymns of Isaac Watts. That hymnbook had revolutionized congregational singing in the English-speaking world. When Watts was born in 1674, congregational singing was either non-existent or, in Calvinist churches, consisted mostly of a rather literal rendering of the Psalms. Watts paraphrased the Psalms and other Scripture passages, reading them through the eyes of the cross.

I used the book devotionally, reading a few hymns each day. I was blessed, not only because of Watts' insight into Scripture, but because of the beauty of his poetry, which praised God and affirmed the faith. I also found some surprises. The books of the Bible on which Watts most frequently based his hymns (besides the Psalms) were not the Gospels but Isaiah (twenty hymns), Revelation (eighteen hymns), and, believe it or not, Song of Solomon (thirteen hymns).

The poems are full of references to angels, the Father's throne, sinners as worms, glory (a favorite word), Jesus as the Lamb slain and solemn decrees.

But even as I read I was aware that Watts' hymns were different from "Methodist hymns," the hymns of the Wesleys and the American camp meetings. When I began doing word studies on hymns, I realized the difference could be epitomized in the use of one word, the word "come." It was not a favorite word with Watts, and he almost always used it to appeal to those who are already Christians.

> *Come, we that love the Lord,*
> *and let our joys be known.*
> *(UMH #733)*

But in hymns by Wesley and other Methodists, the word "come" is usually an invitation to sinners.

> *Come, weary sinners, come,*
> *groaning beneath your load;*
> *the Savior calls his wanderers home;*
> *haste to your pardoning God.*
> (Charles Wesley)

> *Come, every soul by sin oppressed,*
> *there's mercy with the Lord.*
> *(UMH #337)*

Of course! The invitation hymn is a truly Methodist phenomenon. Watts, the Congregationalist, was a Calvinist. Calvinists believe in predestination, that God has decreed who will be saved and who will be lost. This is God's decision, they believe, not ours. God does this so we humans will not boast of our salvation because it is nothing we do. One does not appeal to sinners in Calvinist hymns, because that would imply that they, not God, make the decision about (and thus control) their salvation.

Despite John and Charles Wesley's great love for Calvinists (their good friend George Whitefield eventually broke with them over Calvinism), the Methodist read Scripture differently. When Scripture said, "Come all ye who labor and are heavy laden . . ." the Methodists believed that meant all could be saved. None was too sinful, too poor or too unworthy to merit God's love and his offer of salvation.

Unlimited Atonement (Prevenient Grace)

Today we identify this doctrine or teaching—that none is too unworthy to merit God's offer of salvation—with the idea of "prevenient grace." In historic Methodist terminology it is also linked with the emphasis on "unlimited atonement," "free grace" and, more recently, "free will" or "the dignity of all persons."

Though we are born in sin (Original Sin) and unable to please God by our own efforts, God's Spirit nevertheless seeks us. Christ died on the cross for all persons, and one of the benefits of his death (the Atonement) is the free gift of "prevenient grace" (grace which goes before), a spark that enables us to respond to God's offer of salvation. Therefore, we are important. We matter. God loves us—all of us. Not just the high and mighty. Not just the rich. Not just the people from fine homes with social breeding. Christ died for even—and especially—the poor, the lame, the blind and the otherwise forgotten ones.

The doctrine of free grace relates to each of us personally. It is not God's will that I be lost. Christ died for me, and if I spurn him, I allow him "to die in vain" (a favorite Wesley phrase).

A number of Methodist hymns express this idea. Perhaps the best example is Charles Wesley's hymn based on the great banquet story in Luke 14:16-24 (UMH #339):

> *Come, sinners, to the gospel feast;*
> *let every soul be Jesus' guest.*
> *You need not one be left behind,*
> *for God hath bid all humankind.*
>
> *Sent by my Lord, on you I call,*
> *the invitation is to all.*
> *Come, all the world! Come, sinner, thou!*
> *All things in Christ are ready now.*
>
> *Come, all ye souls by sin oppressed,*
> *ye restless wanderers after rest;*
> *ye poor, and maimed, and halt, and blind,*
> *in Christ a hearty welcome find.*
>
> *My message as from God receive;*
> *ye all may come to Christ and live.*
> *O let his love your hearts constrain,*
> *nor suffer him to die in vain.*
>
> *This is the time; no more delay!*
> *This is the Lord's accepted day.*
> *Come thou, this moment, at his call,*
> *and live for him who died for all.*

Perhaps no other hymn expresses so well the United Methodist idea of unlimited atonement, free grace or prevenient grace. The hymn makes eight references to "all" or "every." The word "come" appears six times. Words like "welcome," "invitation" and "call" (later this is linked with "altar call") appear, as well as the Wesley idea that if we refuse Christ, Christ's death was in vain.

"Come, Sinners, to the Gospel Feast" was one of the most popular Wesley hymns on the American frontier. Almost as popular was Joseph Hart's "Come, Ye Sinners, Poor and Needy" (UMH #340) which conveys the same idea:

> *Come, ye sinners, poor and needy,*
> *weak and wounded, sick and sore;*
> *Jesus ready stands to save you,*
> *full of pity, love and power.*

Following these beloved hymns, Methodists churned out invitation hymns by the thousands, contributing to the spread of revivalism in both England and America. Revivalism assumes that a person can respond to an invitation, and Methodists were among the first to express this in doctrinal form. This teaching became so widespread and commonly accepted that it effectively de-Calvinized many who otherwise claimed to believe in predestination (including Baptists, even if they don't like to admit it).

If this United Methodist distinctive is seldom referred to today, it is only because this belief is so commonly accepted by most groups it no longer seems different or unusual. Christ died for all persons; therefore, all persons can be saved. God's prevenient grace through Christ's death on the cross makes our response possible.

Salvation by Grace through Faith (Justifying Grace)

Salvation by grace through faith is a truth that is by no means unique to the United Methodist tradition. Baptists also affirm this, as do Lutherans. It was one of the key doctrines that led to the Reformation and the establishment of Protestantism. But even Roman Catholics today affirm this truth (at least their interpretation of it). Salvation by grace through faith is the essence of Christianity. It is what the gospel (good news) is all about. We do not need to be lost in our sin. When we respond by faith to God's offer of salvation through the death of Christ, we are "justified," or accepted as righteous.

Still, the Wesleyan revival poured new life into this old doctrine. For early Methodists, both in England and in America, faith was not formal assent to a creed (confessionalism). Nor was it being rightly related to the church (churchianity) or relying primarily on the sacraments (catholicism). Faith was confidence and trust in the crucified and risen Christ. Faith was responding to God's invitation.

This theme is repeated over and over in hymns by Wesley and other early Methodist hymn writers. One of the best examples is found in the hymn "And Can It Be" (UMH #363). The verses outline God's plan of salvation.

1. How can we know God? Why does our Lord care enough for us to die for us? The motive is love.

> *And can it be that I should gain*
> *an interest in the Savior's blood?*
> *Died he for me, who caused his pain?*
> *For me? who him to death pursued?*
> *Amazing love! How can it be*
> *that thou, my God, shouldst die for me?*

2. God has a plan and design so wonderful that not even the angels understand it fully. Again, we praise God because the motive behind the plan is love.

> *'Tis mystery all: Th' Immortal dies!*
> *Who can explore his strange design?*
> *In vain the firstborn seraph tries*
> *to sound the depths of love divine!*
> *'Tis mercy all! Let earth adore;*
> *let angel minds inquire no more.*

3. In this great plan Christ emptied himself and was obedient unto death (see Philippians 2:8). Christ's death was for everyone (Adam's race), and it specifically seeks me out (the suggestion of prevenient grace).

> *He left his Father's throne above,*
> *(so free, so infinite his grace!)*
> *emptied himself of all but love,*
> *and bled for Adam's helpless race.*
> *'Tis mercy all, immense and free,*
> *for O my God, it found out me.*

4. As a consequence of Christ's sacrifice, God's love breaks through to us. The benefit of the cross is that sin's chain is broken (the imagery is from the story of Peter's escape from prison in Acts 12.) True liberation (freedom to love and follow Christ) occurs.

Long my imprisoned spirit lay
fast bound in sin and nature's night;
thine eye diffused a quickening ray;
I woke, the dungeon flamed with light;
my chains fell off, my heart was free,
I rose, went forth, and followed thee.

5. I am justified, or made righteous (the imagery is from Romans 8:1). I need not fear judgment because I have been saved from the consequences of my sin by grace through faith.

No condemnation now I dread,
Jesus, and all in him, is mine;
alive in him, my living Head,
and clothed in righteousness divine,
bold I approach th'eternal throne,
and claim the crown, through Christ my own.

Salvation by grace through faith has been a United Methodist emphasis from the days of Wesley. It is the truth that faith and faith alone is the response that leads to God's justifying grace and our salvation.

Holiness (Sanctifying Grace)

O for a heart to praise my God,
a heart from sin set free,
a heart that always feels thy blood
so freely shed for me.
(UMH #417)

Breathe, O breathe thy loving Spirit
into every troubled breast!
Let us all in thee inherit;
let us find that second rest.
(UMH #384)

Of all the doctrines associated with United Methodism, none affected the American church scene like the doctrine of holiness.

When Charles Wesley used phrases like "a heart from sin set free" and "second rest" (that phrase is changed in some evangelical hymnals to "promised rest"), he was using Methodist family language for "holiness." Other traditional words and phrases for this doctrine include Christian perfection, entire sanctification, Pentecostal experience, the infilling of the Holy Spirit, full salvation, the second blessing—all refer to the teaching that God's Spirit can cleanse us from sin and set us apart to live completely for him.

> *O come, and dwell in me,*
> *Spirit of power within,*
> *and bring the glorious liberty*
> *from sorrow, fear, and sin.*
> *(UMH #388)*

In current United Methodist terminology, the doctrine of holiness is conveyed with the phrase "sanctifying grace." As with other forms of God's grace, sanctifying grace is available to us because of the Atonement, Christ's death on the cross. Prevenient grace prepares us for salvation; justifying grace pardons or justifies or "saves" us; sanctifying grace cleanses, purifies and makes us holy. The word "sanctify" means to "set aside," to "cleanse" or "to make holy."

> *Refining fire, go through my heart,*
> *illuminate my soul;*
> *scatter thy life through every part*
> *and sanctify the whole.*
> *(UMH #422)*

Why is this doctrine so distinctively Methodist? Other groups contemporary with Wesley taught the importance of holy living. Other groups emphasized the work of the Holy Spirit (though there was much less talk then than now about the Holy Spirit). Other groups proclaimed that all of life should be motivated by love. But Methodists went further and taught an optimistic grace in which nothing is impossible with God.

> *Finish, then, thy new creation;*
> *pure and spotless let us be.*
> *Let us see thy great salvation*
> *perfectly restored in thee.*
> *(UMH #384)*

Is there sin in my life? God's grace working through faith can not only forgive it, but eradicate it. Is there sin in society? God's grace working through faith can overcome it (this is why United Methodists have been at the forefront of social justice issues). Are miracles possible? Yes, by God's grace working through faith.

Holiness was a major theme in many early Methodist revivals and camp meetings. It blended well with the then prevailing postmillennialism, the belief that not only individuals but all society would be saved before Christ's return to earth. If God's grace was unlimited, then all evil—including slavery, alcohol and ignorance—was earmarked for defeat. Grace itself was a free gift of God, and zeal for good works was a consequence. The founding of hospitals and schools, concern for the poor, freeing of slaves, honesty in personal dealings—these were ways the faith was meant to be implemented. God's people would not be satisfied until the earth was covered with righteousness.

> *Till all the world shall learn your love*
> *and follow where your feet have trod,*
> *till, glorious from your heaven above,*
> *shall come the city of our God!*
> *(UMH #427)*

In *The United Methodist Hymnal* the section entitled "Sanctifying and Perfecting Grace" covers the topics of "prayer," "trust," "hope" and "strength in tribulation." Anything that helps us to "grow in grace" and become more Christlike is a part of the sanctifying work of the Holy Spirit.

However, holiness as taught in United Methodism today is only a weak substitute for holiness as it was preached in early Methodism. There are several reasons for this.

Unfortunately, holiness in some instances became linked with perfectionism, a concept that seemed to foster a holier-than-thou attitude. Holiness was also identified with a "holy-roller" element whose enthusiasm seemed much too excessive for a Methodism growing affluent. The attempt to suppress the doctrine of holiness was a major reason a large portion of its enthusiasts deserted Methodism from 1880 through 1910. The doctrine lives on in holiness and charismatic groups today—the Assemblies of God, Church of the Nazarene, Salvation Army, Church of God in Christ and in some Pentecostal groups.

Perhaps the time has come to take a new look at this aspect of our heritage. The moral malaise of our times cries out for dedicated, holy living. A new awareness of the doctrine of the Holy Spirit, brought about in part by the charismatic movement, can help us appreciate the spiritual power available to Christians by the outpouring of God's sanctifying grace.

Many of the invitation hymns Methodists wrote for camp meetings and revivals were not so much appeals for sinners to accept Christ (justifying grace), as they were invitations for Christians to yield completely to Christ and receive the Holy Spirit, thus experiencing the power of sanctifying grace. One of these old favorites has been added to *The United Methodist Hymnal.*

All to Jesus I surrender;
all to him I freely give;
I will ever love and trust him,
in his presence daily live.

All to Jesus I surrender;
now I feel the sacred flames.
O the joy of full salvation!
Glory, glory to his name!
(UMH #354)

Many other holiness hymns written by Methodists can be found in old camp meeting and Sunday school hymnals. There are still enough hymns in our present hymnal, however, to remind us of this important part of our United Methodist tradition.

Assurance

United Methodist theology is "Spirit-centered" instead of "word-centered" or "sacrament-centered." It does not focus on creeds, theological systems or church traditions, but rather on the immediate awareness of God's grace. In positive terms: United Methodists believe we can experience Jesus Christ in our hearts.

This means we have a "know so" rather than a "think so" religion.

Blessed assurance, Jesus is mine!
O, what a foretaste of glory divine!
Heir of salvation, purchase of God,
born of his Spirit, washed in his blood. (UMH #369)

While the doctrine of assurance is linked with feeling, emotion and experience, it is incorrect to say this doctrine is *only* about feeling, emotion or experience. One of the most oft-quoted passages of Scripture by the Wesleys was Romans 8:15b-16: "And by him we cry, '*Abba*, Father.' The Spirit himself testifies with our spirit that we are God's children."

In John Wesley's words, there is "an inward impression on the soul, whereby the Spirit of God immediately and directly witnesses to my spirit, that I am a child of God; that Jesus Christ hath loved me, and given Himself for me; that all my sins are blotted out, and I, even I am reconciled to God" (from Wesley's sermon, "Witness of the Spirit").

Perhaps the best example of a hymn that speaks to the doctrine of Assurance is Wesley's "How Can We Sinners Know?" (UMH #372).

How can we sinners know
our sins on earth forgiven?
How can my gracious Savior show
my name inscribed in heaven?

What we have felt and seen,
with confidence we tell,
and publish to the ends of earth
the signs infallible.

We who in Christ believe
that he for us hath died,
we all his unknown peace receive
and feel his blood applied.

We by his Spirit prove
and know the things of God,
the things which freely of his love
he hath on us bestowed.

Our nature's turned, our mind
transformed in all its powers,
and both the witnesses are joined,
the Spirit of God with ours.

Note the "assurance" words and phrases in the hymn: know,

show, felt, seen, confidence, signs, unknown peace receive, felt his blood applied, and by his Spirit prove.

The preaching of assurance gave rise to the early Methodists' characteristic happiness and joy. Instead of suggesting somberness and a dour spirit, a "know so" religion led to emotional outbursts and exuberance. Early camp meeting books are filled with choruses that go something like,

> *Do you know what makes me happy, happy?*
> *Do you know what makes me happy, happy?*
> *Do you know what makes me happy, happy?*
> *There is glory in my soul.*

If our preaching and teaching today is not as specific about the doctrine of Assurance as it was in early Methodism, it is not because the doctrine has fallen into disfavor. Rather, it is because a large portion of the evangelical world has come to take the doctrine for granted. Christians of many traditions today can speak of an "inner witness" or an "assurance" of Christ's love and forgiveness.

Thus, a person like Horatio G. Spafford, though he was not a Methodist, could write about "peace" and "assurance" even after a tragic shipwreck caused the death of five of his daughters. His well-known gospel hymn has been added to the new United Methodist hymnal (UMH #377).

> *When peace, like a river, attendeth my way,*
> *when sorrows like sea billows roll;*
> *whatever my lot, thou hast taught me to say,*
> *it is well, it is well with my soul.*
>
> *Though Satan should buffet, though trials should come,*
> *let this blest assurance control,*
> *that Christ has regarded my helpless estate,*
> *and hath shed his own blood for my soul.*
>
> *It is well with my soul,*
> *it is well, it is well with my soul.*

To Do

A number of beliefs or doctrines still have not been discussed in our chapters on essentials and distinctive emphases. On the basis of the following hymns, how would you interpret Methodist teachings on:

1. Holy Communion

"You Satisfy the Hungry Heart" (UMH #629)

"This Is the Feast of Victory" (UMH #638)

"O the Depth of Love Divine" (UMH #627)

"Let All Mortal Flesh Keep Silence" (UMH #626)

"Come, Sinners, to the Gospel Feast [Communion]" (UMH #616)

2. Satan

"A Mighty Fortress Is Our God" (UMH #110)

"Onward, Christian Soldiers," (UMH #575, vv. 1,2)

"Break Forth, O Beauteous Heavenly Light," (UMH #223, v. 1)

"Soldiers of Christ, Arise" (poem) (UMH #513)

"'Tis Finished! The Messiah Dies" (UMH #282)

Fourteen

Looking at the Church's Diversity

The Christian family contains various theological, sociological, ethnic, denominational and even geographical subcultures. We serve a common Lord, but we differ in how we worship and express our faith.

United Methodism is one part of the body of Christ, but even United Methodism has its subgroupings: liberal and evangelical, urban and rural, ethnic, East coast and Midwest, North American and African. In addition, Methodism is different today than it was fifty years ago, or two hundred years ago.

A study of the language and images of different types of hymns can tell us about some of the differences among these subgroups. Before giving a final prognosis on the future of United Methodism, it might be helpful to share the results of a study that was conducted to discover (1) theological differences in several types of hymns, (2) the theological shifts that have taken place as evidenced in the hymns and (3) the extent to which each is a continuation of our Wesleyan past.

The study selected five types of hymns and noted the kind of language and imagery used in those hymns. Each category has approximately one hundred hymns. The five types are:

1. The hymns of Wesley. If it is true that the hymns of the Wesleys set the tone for the style and theology of Methodism, it should be worthwhile to note what the Wesley hymns were about.

Eighty Wesley hymns originally chosen for inclusion in *The United Methodist Hymnal* were used in the study (about seventy of these actually found their way into the hymnal).

2. Gospel hymns from the Sankey era. One hundred hymns were randomly selected from Sankey's *Gospel Hymns No. 1 to 6*. These are what many people today know as "the old hymns." They date from the late 1800s and include a large percentage of hymns by women and Methodists.

3. Hymns of the social gospel era. All of the hymns written in the last one hundred years (or from about 1885) that appeared in the 1935 and/or 1966 Methodist hymnal but which were deleted from *The United Methodist Hymnal* are included in this group. These hymns are discussed in chapter seven. They were introduced into the hymnals because they were, at the time, contemporary and relevant and their themes (peace and justice and brotherhood) were being emphasized by the theology of the day. This group contains 109 hymns.

4. Contemporary ecumenical hymns. These hymns were written since the last Methodist hymnal in the mid-1960s (none are ethnic or gospel hymns) which are included in *The United Methodist Hymnal*. These are the "new" hymns. Some were actually commissioned to fill in gaps where it was determined that new images or new emphases (such as peace and justice) or new ways of expressing our faith are needed. There are one hundred hymns in this group, including the hymns of such highly regarded authors as Fred Pratt Green, Brian Wren and Fred Kaan.

5. Contemporary gospel hymns. This group contains ninety-five hymns written within the last thirty years which were taken from an independent evangelical hymnal, Word Publisher's *The Hymnal for Worship and Celebration*. These are hymns by persons such as Bill and Gloria Gaither, Ralph Carmichael and John Peterson. They include several choruses (Word's hymnal contains an additional one hundred or so choruses) and represent the kind of music being sung in many evangelical churches, including a number of United Methodist churches, today.

THE NUMBER OF TIMES SELECTED WORDS OR PHRASES APPEAR WITHIN THE TEXT OF EACH GROUP OF HYMNS

	Wesley	Sankey	Social Gospel	Ecumenical Contemporary	Evangelical Contemporary
Father	16	17	24	7	25
Jesus	60	148	13	33	126
Lamb of God	10	4	1	5	24
Master	4	10	17	0	5
King	14	34	29	1	27
Christ	26	22	31	83	38
God of...	0	0	30	34	1
Savior	26	58	18	4	36
Spirit, or Holy Spirit	25	6	14	44	32
Creator, creation	2	1	4	20	8
brotherhood	0	0	12	0	0
blood (of Jesus)	31	27	0	7	9
Christ dies for...	20	15	4	3	12
tears	7	18	1	0	0
Name, or Name of (Jesus)	36	13	2	7	62
sin, or sinner	81	55	11	13	20
truth	17	7	32	18	5
beauty	0	0	7	0	0
heaven	32	7	2	0	2
peace	10	21	33	39	4
glory	32	29	32	9	41
Come, as an invitation	16	47	1	0	0
Hymns with a clear reference to the Atonement	25	33	0	4	17

Some Observations

Wesley Hymns

One cannot study the Wesley hymns without sensing the power that launched the Great Evangelical Revival in England, the Great Awakening in America, and Methodism. These are hymns like "O For a Thousand Tongues to Sing," "Jesus, Lover of My Soul" and "And Can It Be that I Should Gain an Interest In the Savior's Blood." They are "Hark! the Herald Angels Sing," "I Want a Principle Within" and "Love Divine, All Loves Excelling."

While the hymns address many subjects, their overriding theme is the good news of Jesus Christ's death on the cross as an atonement for sin, and the salvation that is ours by faith because of that sacrifice. There is continual exaltation of Jesus Christ. The love of Jesus reaches out to us; the blood of Jesus saves us. It is the name of Jesus that is lifted up. To Jesus belong power and glory and honor.

Wesley hymns reflect early Methodist preaching and practice. The doctrines of free grace, Assurance and perfect love are found there. There is frequent appeal to sinners. A key word is "come," an invitation to accept the salvation offered in Jesus Christ.

The Wesley hymns have done much to define modern evangelicalism. They have also served, though unofficially, as doctrinal standards for Methodism. Even in Methodism's darkest hours, when various forms of modern theology strove to accommodate the faith to the secular world and thus distort its original vision, the Wesley hymns called us back to our roots.

The new hymnal has greatly strengthened the Wesley corpus by printing the entire text of several key hymns, including "O for a Thousand Tongues to Sing" (UMH #57), "Soldiers of Christ, Arise" (UMH #513), "Sinners, Turn: Why Will You Die?" (UMH #346) and "Come, O Thou Traveler Unknown" (UMH #387). The extra verses in these hymns are printed as poetry, with the hope that they will be used devotionally for their insights into the nature of the faith we proclaim.

Wesley hymns no longer dominate the singing of United Methodists. Many of the tunes are from another era. They are not well suited for those churches not trained to think theologically, or that select music primarily for its entertainment value.

But these hymns still represent a standard by which all other hymns can be judged, both in their poetry and their theology. One of the best arguments for using *The United Methodist Hymnal* instead of other evangelical hymnals is its rich supply of Wesley material. Here Wesleys' writings capture the essence of the biblical faith in a way few other hymnals do.

Gospel Hymns

I once spoke about hymnology in a country United Methodist church and asked the twenty-five people present to name their favorite hymns. When they were finished, I pointed out that every one of their twenty-five responses was a gospel hymn written by an American between 1870 and 1920. Their favorites included "The Old Rugged Cross," "Blessed Assurance," "In the Garden," "When the Roll Is Called Up Yonder" and "Sing the Wondrous Love of Jesus."

These are the "old favorites" that many people like to sing. Interestingly, they are sung by people around the world. Missionaries tell of the surprising popularity of American gospel songs in Africa, South America and Asia. They are sung by all ethnic groups. Long after their predicted demise, these hymns still touch a responsive chord in the hearts of many believers.

But why do they dominate the musical preferences of so many people, even today? The poetry is, after all, often atrocious. The tunes are predictable and repetitious. Why had none of the people in that country church selected a Wesley hymn, a contemporary hymn by the Gaithers or any of the hymns associated with formal worship as a favorite hymn?

After a long discussion I offered an answer to my own question. The little country church was nearly one hundred years old. It was a family church and many of the people present were descendants of some of the first members. The music they sang and preferred was the music under which their parents and grandparents had been converted. It was music that had helped shape that church. It was shared history. In a sense, it was their understanding of United Methodism. New songs and other songs were all right. But their favorites were the hymns that linked them to their past and helped them identify who they were.

Gospel music from the Ira Sankey and Homer Rodeheaver era is Wesley music that was reworked by camp meetings, the

American frontier, Sunday schools and big city revivals. Like Wesley music it is concerned, sometimes overly so, with salvation; it is directed to Jesus; it is experiential, with the Atonement being a key theme; and it is often addressed to sinners. Whatever the weaknesses of gospel music (and there are many), it is in the lineage of the Wesleys. In large part, it has defined and been defined by modern evangelicalism. It is the music of choice for many believers.

Hymns of the Social Gospel

These hymns have already been discussed in chapter seven. What is worth mentioning again is the discontinuity between the theology behind these hymns and historic Methodism. Very few of these hymns are addressed to Jesus. Jesus is seen as an example, but almost never as Savior or Lord.

The theology of these hymns posits grace without atonement and a Christianity without a cross. This group contains no invitation hymns addressed to sinners, mostly because persons are not seen as sinners or "lost" in the first place. These hymns place a strong emphasis on living and doing the faith, with many references to truth, beauty, strength, bravery and compassion. At the same time, no judgment is mentioned for those who do not meet God's high standards.

Hymns of the social gospel had their greatest success in the period from 1900-1935, the period of liberal optimism. God's kingdom would come to earth if his people would all try harder and follow the example of Jesus. The idealism of these hymns moved many people to action, and not a few souls were won for the cause of Christ because of them.

But the idealism was difficult to sustain. The Great Depression and World War II destroyed much of the optimism that was based, in large part, on human effort. Liberalism itself moved on to other ventures.

A number of these hymns have been retained in the new United Methodist hymnal. (The study of social gospel hymns was done only on those that were removed.) Of those included some are United Methodist favorites: "Are Ye Able," "God of Grace and God of Glory" and "O Young and Fearless Prophet," to name a few. These are the hymns many of us grew up with in Sunday school and church camp.

By themselves, these hymns are a weak representation of the gospel. Used along with other hymns, however, they will continue to serve the church well.

Ecumenical Contemporary

A major reason for hymnal revision is to take advantage of new tunes and new texts that have been written in the last twenty-five years. The revision committee considered several thousand hymns, many never before published, for inclusion in *The United Methodist Hymnal*. Some were commissioned especially for the hymnal.

A diversity of contemporary hymns was selected for final inclusion. *The United Methodist Hymnal* can rightfully claim to offer something for everyone. The new hymns include evangelical songs, praise choruses and ethnic-background hymns, as well as many texts that represent what might be called "liberalism updated." These are hymns selected for their relevance to the new age, in the tradition of the social gospel hymns of the earlier part of the century.

It is the latter group that was studied for its use of languages and images. One hundred hymns in *The United Methodist Hymnal* were chosen because they address contemporary concerns in contemporary language. Their topics include wholeness, healing, women's images, spiritual formation, liberation, inclusiveness and peace with justice.

Several of these hymns were written by United Methodists, including "What Gift Can We Bring" (UMH #87) by Jane Marshall, "God, Whose Love Is Reigning O'er Us" (UMH #100) by William Boyd Grove, "How Like a Gentle Spirit" (UMH #115) by C. Eric Lincoln and "In the Bulb There Is a Flower" (UMH #707) by Natalie Sleeth.

The first thing to note about these hymns is that they have been introduced to the church with a great deal of excitement. It is hoped that these hymns might influence the worship of the church for the next several generations. Hymns were discussed by the Hymnal Revision Committee in light of what the church would be thinking and singing in the twenty-first century.

However, it is possible that more may be expected of these hymns than they can deliver. "Relevant" and "contemporary" hymns in the liberal or mainline tradition have not fared well in recent years. The question is not whether such hymns are worthy, but whether they can claim to belong to a larger spiritual movement. Have any of these hymns given identity to United Methodists or mobilized and inspired the church for mission or been identified with renewal?

It can be argued that since the great social gospel hymns of the 1920s, few, if any, hymns from the liberal perspective have become favorites among United Methodists or the larger Christian community. Most of the new hymns introduced in the 1964 hymnal now lie forgotten and discarded. The church usage rate (the percentage of United Methodist churches that actually use a hymn) of the fifty hymns (not counting gospel, spirituals or Christmas songs) that were introduced in 1964 and carried over to the new hymnal averages twenty-two percent. The church usage rate for gospel hymns and Negro spirituals introduced in the 1964 hymnal and retained in the 1989 hymnal averages seventy-seven percent.

Perhaps the story will be different for the ecumenical contemporary hymns introduced in the 1989 hymnal. A number of the hymns touch a responsive chord in many of us. Several are faithful expositions of biblical passages.

Having said this, we must still ask if these hymns as a whole are in continuity with Wesleyan theology, and whether they trigger the spiritual sensitivities of most United Methodists.

Comparing one hundred of these hymns with the 109 social gospel hymns studied reveals that some rather interesting shifts have occurred over the past sixty years in the way we speak about God and the faith. The new hymns have fewer references to Father and King and Master and many more references to Creator and Spirit. Gone is talk about kingdom building and the Fatherhood of God and the Brotherhood of Man. It has been replaced with images of freeing, nurturing, healing and mothering.

From an evangelical perspective, the hymns, like the social gospel hymns that preceded them, have very little to say about what many Christians always assumed is the essence of the faith: the good news of Christ's death on the cross to atone for our sin, salvation by grace through faith and heaven gained.

There is a reluctance in these hymns to name the Name, that is, to extol Jesus as Savior and Lord. This is probably the biggest difference between contemporary evangelical music (which is mostly gospel) and ecumenical contemporary music. Contemporary evangelical music continually lifts up the name of Jesus, and proclaims Jesus as Lord. In contrast, ecumenical contemporary music almost never exalts Jesus as Lord and uses the word "name" mostly to refer to various names for God. A good example of this is Thomas Troeger's hymn "Source and Sovereign, Rock and Cloud," the refrain of which says,

> *May the church at prayer recall*
> *that no single holy name*
> *but the truth behind them all*
> *is the God whom we proclaim.*
> *(UMH #113)*

The hymn seems to express well certain liberal sentiments: 1) metaphors and names are one and the same, and one name is as valid as another since God is greater than them all (this presumably includes names like Allah and Buddha); 2) traditional language such as Father, Master or Lord can be replaced with non-sexist references that are just as meaningful; 3) God-talk is preferable to Jesus-talk. This may be good liberalism. The question is whether it is good Christianity.

Related to this—and part of the larger issue of how are we to talk about God—is the high number of references (thirty-four in the ecumenical-contemporary hymns) to "God of. . . ." In the hymns studied, we have God of many names—God of the sparrow, God of the whale, God of ancient glory, God of the pruning hook, God of Jewish faith, God of change and glory, God of many signs—most of which obscure rather than clarify the distinction between God and the world.

This "God of . . ." language is common in mysticism and/or pantheistic faiths, which see God as in everything, and not identified with particular people, places or times. In contrast, the historic Christian faith sees God especially identified in Jesus Christ, in the cross and in the events of the Scriptures.

Another unfortunate trend in the ecumenical-contemporary hymns is what might be called the de-personalizing of God. Much of this results from the attempt to rid contemporary hymns of all sexist language regarding God. God is rarely ever referred to as "he" or "him" in the hymns. Much modern theology argues that

God is beyond personality. But to be beyond personality sounds a great deal like being reduced to force or power or creative energy. Such theology does not have much problem with the Incarnation, that is, that God was in Christ. When God is seen primarily as an impersonal force, God is incarnate in a lot of things. But suspicion about the de-personalizing of God becomes greater when one notes the number of references in these hymns to God as womb, hovering wings, birth of time, endlessly becoming, love's cosmic mind, energies that never tire, of life, whole life, all life endowed. Related to this is a lack of references to God (or Christ) as Lord, Master, Father or King.

This is not to say that the ecumenical-contemporary hymns in *The United Methodist Hymnal* are bad hymns or are to be avoided. Not all these hymns should be classified as "liberal." The hymns of Fred Pratt Green, for example, contain fairly traditional theology. But by themselves, these hymns present an uncertain gospel. Some of these hymns will find an important place in the United Methodism of the future. Some will become favorites. As supplemental hymns, used alongside the many fine hymns in the hymnal, they will serve the church well.

Contemporary Gospel

I once attended the Gaither Praise Gathering. It was a combination music festival, publisher's promotional event and evangelical family reunion. Sandi Patti was there, as were Bill and Gloria Gaither, the Brooklyn Tabernacle Choir and ten thousand others. It was an ecumenical gathering, attracting Mennonites, Baptists, United Methodists and Roman Catholics. But it was not part of what is called the "ecumenical movement," which refers mostly to exclusively mainline, delegated activities.

The Praise Gathering and events like charismatic meetings, Bible conferences, city-wide evangelistic crusades and a swirl of ministries related to parachurch groups are a part of what might be called the evangelical subculture or the evangelical movement. The evangelical movement is not in any way organized, but it has its own heroes (Billy Graham), its own seminaries (Fuller, Asbury, Trinity), its own periodicals (*Christianity Today*) and its own media (Christian radio and television). At one time Methodism personified the evangelical movement. Today, despite

Methodism's liberal image, a large portion of the denomination could still be classified as evangelical.

The Praise Gathering offered speakers, worship and seminars. But what attracted people was the music: choirs, artists, groups and lots of singing. Most of the music was gospel: contemporary, southern, black and traditional.

Gospel music traces its lineage back through Thomas Dorsey, Homer Rodeheaver, Fanny Crosby, Ira Sankey, the frontier revival, camp meetings, the Wesleys and Isaac Watts. Along the way it absorbed elements of whatever was the popular music of the day, whether folk music, tavern songs, plantation work songs, the blues or rock and roll. In its earlier days it was often identified with the Methodist movement. Gospel music has, to a large extent, defined evangelicalism today.

Gospel music dominates the music played on Christian radio today. It is the music sold in Christian book stores. It is also the music most closely identified with many of the growing churches and denominations across the country. Gospel music is now a money-making business, complete with star artists, record companies, concerts and awards. It is obviously more than worship music. It is also entertainment.

Some observations based on results of the study of contemporary gospel music are in order.

1. The chorus is a very important part of contemporary gospel. These are sometimes called Scripture songs, worship choruses, praise songs or even charismatic choruses. Choruses have not changed much since the days of Methodist camp meetings, when they were introduced in an outdoor setting where there were no instruments and few hymn books. These songs are simple and easily memorized.

There is a place for the chorus. Unfortunately, choruses by themselves provide very little religious substance. They deal with images, not theological subtleties presented poetically. They lack the profound affirmations of classic hymns.

Several choruses are included in the 1989 United Methodist hymnal. Among these are "El Shaddai" (UMH #123), "Jesus, Jesus, Jesus" (UMH #171) and "Majesty, Worship His Majesty" (UMH #176).

2. Contemporary gospel, along with almost all contemporary

Christian music, places a much greater emphasis on the Holy Spirit than in the past. Despite the fact that Methodism was a Holy Spirit movement, there were few references to the Holy Spirit in camp meeting music or in early gospel music.

3. The lifting up of Jesus and the name of Jesus is still a central focus of contemporary gospel. The contrast between gospel music and liberal music in the number of references to Jesus is marked. Contemporary gospel also continues earlier gospel music's emphasis on the death of Jesus Christ for the sins of the world (Atonement) and the testimony to the new birth.

At the same time, contemporary gospel places less emphasis on the invitation aspect of the gospel message as symbolized by the use of the word "come." Contemporary gospel is still addressed in part to sinners (five such hymns were identified in the study) but it is more preachy and less compassionate than Wesley or early gospel. As an indication of this, references to "tears," an image that characterized Sankey's gospel music, are gone.

4. Compared to earlier gospel music, contemporary gospel uses fewer images of pilgrims in the barren land or sailors lost at sea. It places less emphasis on heaven and doesn't make as many references to blood or even to sinners. It pays much more attention to the second coming of Christ and stresses worship, especially worship that ascribes glory, majesty and power to the name of Jesus.

Common people have always appreciated gospel music more than trained musicians do. It has often been used to penetrate secular culture. Many young Christians today entered the Christian faith through contemporary gospel. It is the kind of music recommended for churches who want to reach teenagers and young adults. However, contemporary gospel is only a partial witness to the fullness of historic faith. It is best used as a supplement, rather than a replacement, to traditional music.

The United Methodist Hymnal includes several of the contemporary gospel songs that were used in the study. Some of these are: "Because He Lives," "He Touched Me" and "Something Beautiful," by Bill and Gloria Gaither; and "My Tribute" (chorus only) by Andrae Crouch. In addition, a number of traditional gospel songs have been included, bringing the number of evangelical hymns in the hymnal to approximately two hundred. This is the first time gospel music has been a significant part of an official hymnal.

Is There Hope for the Church?

What can be done to revitalize United Methodism? I remember an interview at the North Central Jurisdictional Conference. An episcopal candidate was asked what she would do to reverse the membership decline in the church.

Her response: "We need to removementalize the church."

Heads nodded approvingly. Whether we understood it or not, it was spoken authoritatively and impressively. Then someone, less reserved than the rest of us, had the courage to ask, "What does removementalize mean?"

"We must become a movement again," was the answer. "Movementalize" means to "make a movement," so removementalize means to remake what was once a movement, but now isn't, into a movement again.

Of course. United Methodism today is an institution, a denomination. It is church buildings with tall steeples and seminaries with 400,000-book libraries. It is retirement homes and publishing houses and mission agencies. It is heavily endowed church-related colleges, which have achieved prestige in the academic world (if not the Christian world). United Methodism is a bureaucracy with so many agencies that some (such as Religion and Race and the Role and Status of Women) exist primarily to monitor other agencies. It is an eight hundred page *Discipline* and a *Book of Resolutions* with church positions on every topic from prison reform to Antarctica.

But it is not a movement. A movement, whether organized or not, is characterized by a shared vision, a strong moral stance and common beliefs. A movement has a mission and those who are part of it know what the mission is. A movement has heroes, symbols, a common language; it is family. A movement has its music.

Movements are not the product of planning and management techniques. Movements are not inspired by bureaucracies. Our seminaries, with their sights fixed on respectability and the academic world, will not set any movements in motion.

Religious movements grow out of revival and Great Awakenings. Movements are often accompanied with the rediscovery of scriptural truths long neglected, such as salvation by faith, Christian perfection or the gifts of the Spirit. Movements occur when unreached groups—the poor, the disinherited, clans, tribes, ethnic groups—find new life in Christ and their excitement spreads to others. Perhaps we should not hope for United Methodism to become a movement again, but we should hope instead that groups within the church will find renewal and will bring new life to the whole body.

However renewal comes to the church, music will be an important part of it. It is hard to predict what effect *The United Methodist Hymnal* will have on the church in the next two decades. There are hopeful signs, however, that with its variety of styles of music, its lifting up of important truths of the faith, its inclusiveness toward all groups of people, the hymnal will be a force for good.

That is the prayer of many of us.

To Do

1. Discuss the hymns and the music that have helped shape your faith (which may not always be the same as your favorite hymns). From what kind of background did that music come?

2. Are you willing to sacrifice your allegiance to some old, favorite hymns to make room for new, contemporary hymns in the hymnal?

3. Do you see signs of hope for the United Methodist Church in the new hymnal?

Notes

Four

1. Charles Etherington, *Protestant Worship Music* (New York: Holt, Rinehart and Winston, Inc., 1962), 191.

2. Quoted in John Norman Sims, *The Hymnody of the Camp Meeting Tradition* (Unpublished Manuscript, Union Theological Seminary, 1960), 145-147.

3. Quoted in H. Richard Niebuhr, *The Social Sources of Denominationalism* (New York: Henry Holt and Company, Inc., 1929), 29.

4. James Fry, "The Early Camp Meeting Song Writers," *The Methodist Quarterly Review,* (July, 1859), 407.

5. Theolphilus Armenious, "Account of the Rise and Progress of the Work of God in the Western Country," *The Methodist Quarterly Review,* 304.

6. *The Journal and Letters of Francis Asbury,* Vol. 3 (Nashville: Abingdon Press, 1958), 398.

Five

1. James Fry, "The Early Camp Meeting Song Writers," *The Methodist Quarterly Review* (July, 1859), 405.

2. Ellen Jane Lorenz, *Glory, Hallelujah!* (Nashville: Abingdon, 1978), 134.

3. Richard Wheatley, "The Revised Methodist Hymnal," *Methodist Quarterly Review,* (July, 1879), 527.

4. Louis F. Benson, *The English Hymn* (Philadelphia: The Presbyterian Board of Publications, 1915), 300.

5. Vinson Synan, *The Holiness-Pentecostal Movement in the United States* (Grand Rapids: Eerdman's Publishing Company, 1971), 50.

6. Synan, Op. cit., 77.

Six

1. Quoted in Arthur L. Stevenson, *The Story of Southern Hymnology* (New York: AMS Press, Inc., 1975), 88.

2. This and other quotes are taken from Stevenson, Arthur L., *The Story of Southern Hymnody.* (New York: AMS Press, Inc., 1975), 50-57. The book was originally published in 1931.

Seven

1. For a more complete evaluation of the 1935 hymnal, see: Benjamin Crawford, *Religious Trends in a Century of Hymns* (Carnegie Church Press).

2. Richard Wheatley, "The Revised Methodist Hymnal," *Methodist Quarterly Review,* (1879), 525.

3. O.E. Brown, "Modernism: A Calm Survey." *The Methodist Quarterly Review*, Vol. 74, No. 3, (July, 1925), 399.

4. There are actually 109 such hymns, and they are as follows: From the 1935 hymnal: numbers 10, 33, 78, 79, 99, 101, 123, 131, 145, 152, 158, 160, 294, 295, 300, 308, 331, 361, 365, 368, 391, 395, 406, 421, 425, 433, 445, 448, 457, 461, 463, 464, 467, 468, 470, 473, 478, 494, 495, 497, 504, 506, 508, 510, 521, 555, 556, 558, 559, 560, 562.

From the 1966 hymnal: numbers 6, 11, 19, 44, 47, 57, 141, 171, 188, 189, 190, 191, 194, 197, 198, 201, 202, 203, 206, 225, 243, 260, 273, 321, 349, 350, 351, 356, 362, 370, 371, 377, 408, 411, 422, 442, 449, 456, 460, 469, 475, 476, 481, 482, 485, 486, 490, 506, 512, 514, 517, 519, 525, 532, 534, 541, 546, 548.

Nine

1. Quoted in Dena J. Epstein, *Sinful Tunes and Spirituals* (Urbana: University of Illinois Press, 1977), 105.

2. See Eileen Southern, *The Music of Black Americans* (New York: W.W. Norton & Company, 1983), 77-78, 84.

3. *The Journal and Letters of Francis Asbury.* **September 18, 1797.**

4. J.B.T. Marsh, The Story of the Jubilee Singers; With Their *Songs* (Boston: Houghton, Mifflin and Company, 1880.)

5. Epstein, op. cit., 275.

Ten

1. *Zion's Songsters* (New York: Harper and Brothers, 1830), #253.

2. Harry Emerson Fosdick, *The Manhood of the Master* (New York: Association Press. 1913.)